GRANTSMANSHIP
FOR CRIMINAL
JUSTICE AND
CRIMINOLOGY

Books Under the General Editorship of
DANIEL CURRAN

CRIME AS STRUCTURED ACTION
by *James W. Messerschmidt*

EMERGING CRIMINAL JUSTICE
Three Pillars for a Proactive Justice System
by *Paul H. Hahn*

CRIME CONTROL AND WOMEN
Implications of Criminal Justice Policy
edited by Susan L. Miller

HOW TO RECOGNIZE GOOD POLICING
Problems and Issues
edited by Jean-Paul Brodeur

CRIME AND IMMIGRANT YOUTH
by *Tony Waters*

GRANTSMANSHIP FOR CRIMINAL JUSTICE AND CRIMINOLOGY
by *Mark S. Davis*

GRANTSMANSHIP
FOR CRIMINAL
JUSTICE AND
CRIMINOLOGY

Mark S. Davis

Sage Publications, Inc.
International Educational and Professional Publisher
Thousand Oaks ▪ London ▪ New Delhi

For information:

Sage Publications, Inc.
2455 Teller Road
Thousand Oaks, California 91320
E-mail: order@sagepub.com

Sage Publications Ltd.
6 Bonhill Street
London EC2A 4PU
United Kingdom

Sage Publications India Pvt. Ltd.
M-32 Market
Greater Kailash I
New Delhi 110 048 India

Printed in the United States of America

Library of Congress Cataloging-in-Publication Data

Davis, Mark S., project director
    Grantsmanship for criminal justice and criminology / by Mark S. Davis.
        p.   cm.
    Includes bibliographical references and index.
    ISBN 0-7619-1128-6 (cloth: acid-free paper)
    ISBN 0-7619-1129-4 (paper: acid-free paper)
    1. Criminology—Research grants.   2. Proposal writing for grants.
    I. Title
    HV6024.5 .D39   1999
    364'.079'73—dc21   99–6109

This book is printed on acid-free paper.

00   01   02   03   04   05   06   7   6   5   4   3   2   1

Acquiring Editor:	Kassie Gavrilis
Editorial Assistant:	Anna Howland
Production Editor:	Denise Santoyo
Editorial Assistant:	Patricia Zeman
Designer/Typesetter:	Rose Tylak/Lynn Miyata
Indexer:	Teri Greenberg

Dedication

*I would like to dedicate this book to the thousands
of law enforcement officers, court administrators,
victim advocates, domestic violence shelter workers,
researchers, professors, and others whose careers
either directly or indirectly involve the prevention
and control of crime and delinquency, who,
in addition to their demanding duties, find the
time to write grant applications and proposals.*

Contents

Acknowledgments

There are a number of people to whom I am indirectly indebted. Some of my former and current colleagues at the Ohio Office of Criminal Justice Services have taught me more about grants and grantsmanship than they realize. Especially deserving of thanks are Paul Bronsdon, Melissa Dunn, Jack Harmeyer, Phyllis Hester, Tracy Mahoney, Tom Mallory, D. Jeanne Roberts, and Bob Swisher. Through countless hours of team review, these women and men inculcated in me an appreciation of what constitutes an application worthy of funding. I hope that the many grantees of the Office of Criminal Justice Services appreciate the numerous contributions those people make.

In addition, I acknowledge the hundreds of police officers, sheriff's deputies, victim advocates, judges, court administrators, probation officers, alcohol and drug counselors, and other professionals who enrolled in my grantsmanship courses at the then Cincinnati Private Police Academy, the Criminal Justice Technology and Education Center in Toledo, and the Ohio Peace Officer Training Academy in London, Ohio. In testing these materials with challenging students, I was able to see the need for such a book and eventually to refine the ideas into a manuscript. All these students were eager and attentive, and I hope that they went on to win the grants they needed.

I also would like to thank Terry Hendrix of Sage for his seeing the merits of this book and championing my cause. I will very much miss his enthusiastic support of new ideas. I also greatly appreciate the efforts of Terry's successor, Kassie Gavrilis, who saw the book through to publication. A special thanks is due to Alison Binder, who patiently guided me through the copyediting process.

Introduction

As long as there is crime, there will be grant monies to combat it. Not only is this true in the late 1990s, but it was true 25 years ago, and it will be true 25 years from now. Congress periodically manages to authorize and appropriate millions of dollars for the latest "war against crime," whatever that phrase really means. Most recently, this war manifested itself in the Violent Crime Control and Law Enforcement Act of 1994, a multifaceted piece of legislation designed to strike a balance between tough crime control measures and somewhat softer preventive measures. As these words were being typed, monies from the 1994 act were still flowing for a variety of purposes ranging from putting 100,000 new cops on the street to combating violence against women to providing recreational programs for disadvantaged urban youth.

Whatever one's take is on such legislation or on the motivations behind it, these federal crime bills create innumerable opportunities for criminal justice professionals in need of grant funds. Whether the grant seeker is a university-based researcher who wants to test a theory of crime or a grassroots community organizer who is trying desperately to prevent gang activity in a neighborhood, crime legislation that appropriates grant funds offers the promise of being able to pursue a project that otherwise might be difficult, if not impossible, to undertake.

As soon as these bills become law, federal, state, and local bureaucracies scramble to implement the new grant programs. But eventually, the solicitations go out, and the grant seekers are in business. A single formula grant program in one state can result in literally hundreds of potential grant awards worth tens of millions of dollars. When this is multiplied by the number of federal criminal justice grant programs and then by the number of states and territories, the fund-

ing opportunities for criminal justice professionals across the country become
almost staggering.

Private foundations have also made a strong commitment to funding crime
and justice programs. During the past couple of decades, foundations such as the
Annie E. Casey Foundation, the Edna McConnell Clark Foundation, the Joyce
Foundation, and others have shown considerable interest in innovative practices
designed to address crime, delinquency, and the administration of justice. Although many criminal justice professionals do not automatically think of private
foundations as prospective sponsors, the fields of criminology and criminal justice have benefited greatly from their generosity.

WHY ARE GRANTS SO IMPORTANT?

Criminal justice work goes on with or without grants. A police chief who has no
grant money makes use of whatever local operating funds are available to send
officers out to enforce laws and promote public safety. If the sum needed for a
special project is modest, the chief might approach a service organization or
hold a raffle to raise the money. The chief might also be able meet the need by ac-
quiring surplus military equipment. So the absence of grant monies will not
bring local safety services to a halt.

The same is true for other criminal justice professionals. Without grant funds,
a prosecutor is still obligated to take felony cases to the grand jury and represent
the state's interests in the courts against the accused. The same can be said for all
the other criminal justice professionals whose existences do not depend on grant
money. So why do so many people in the field seem preoccupied with getting
their hands on grant funds?

One of the truisms in criminal justice, as well as in other arenas, is that "my
work will still be there." No matter how hard criminal justice professionals
work, the cases continue, sometimes ebbing, sometimes flowing. But day after
day, there is more than ample evidence that crime is alive and well. For some professionals, this endless barrage of crime prompts a change in career. For others,
it results in cynicism or burnout that turns a once-exciting challenge into a mo-
notonous, repetitive exercise day in and day out until retirement.

But for many criminal justice professionals, this daily dose of human misery
and the frustrations that accompany the processing of it evoke interesting questions. Why couldn't we reduce our backlog of drug cases by processing these offenders a little differently? Why couldn't we discourage gang activity by cleaning up vandalism and other signs of neighborhood neglect? Why can't we reduce
the excessive use of force by police and foster respect for officers by teaching
them to treat citizens with a greater measure of fairness and courtesy? Despite
what we may personally think of such ideas, they come from well-meaning professionals looking for answers to concrete problems.

Innovations in criminal justice and criminology that have shown promise came about in just that way. Creative professionals, including those in criminal justice, tire of repeating the same programs that offer little in the way of insight or change. To upset the status quo, professionals often are forced to find new funds to test these promising new approaches. In time, some of these innovations eventually become common, accepted practice. But in many cases, these innovations would not have happened without the start given them by grant funds.

The same is true for academic criminologists. Professors can, and in some cases may rightly prefer to, analyze secondary data to test their research hypotheses. But in other instances, the research they really want to pursue may necessitate the collection of new data. This most often will require a grant to fund the graduate research associates, travel, equipment, and other expenses associated with what might be an expensive, large-scale research project. Applying for a research grant represents a lot of work, but the chance to break new theoretical or empirical ground may well be worth the time and trouble.

The funding organizations that award grants are interested in these innovative projects. Although they certainly don't want to fund any one program forever, many such organizations are willing to give a direct service program or a research study the start it needs to prove itself. Other grants may promote a recent innovation in the field by helping criminal justice agencies adopt it. Examples of these include grants to promote community policing, mediation programs, drug courts, and community justice.

WHY A BOOK FOR CRIMINAL JUSTICE AND CRIMINOLOGY?

In my many years of working with grants as an applicant, reviewer, and instructor, I have learned that many criminal justice professionals are afraid of writing grants. Some people suffer from math anxiety. Others fear computers so much that they won't experiment with their potential or even turn one on. Writing is another common bogeyman for many of us. And so it is with preparing grant applications or proposals. Law enforcement officers who daily face such dangers as wanted felons and high-speed chases have been known to shrink when faced with a blank grant application that has to be completed. One main purpose of this book, then, is to help strip away the dread and anxiety associated with writing criminal justice grants. By breaking the grant-writing process into its constituent parts, I intend to show that there truly is nothing to fear.

There may be a much more important reason for this book. The allied fields of criminal justice and criminology may well be on the edge of a new paradigm. Far too many criminal justice professionals are dissatisfied with the status quo. Crime control strategies driven by baseball epithets such as "three strikes and you're out" have failed to enamor the majority of those charged with controlling serious and violent crime. The get-tough stance that currently manifests itself in legislation does not seem to be getting a warm welcome from either the academic or practitioner communities. Such dissatisfaction eventually will find its way to legislators. Through some national task force on crime, a series of influential books on the subject, or both, legislators at the federal and state levels will take notice of the need for more effective, more humane methods of crime control. Their eventual response undoubtedly will lead to appropriations to help make any new approach work, whatever form it takes. This book, then, should help those pursuing the next paradigm to support their work through grant funding.

There are corresponding dissatisfactions with the prevention of crime. Despite the well-intentioned efforts of many hard-working professionals, much of what occurs under the rubric of crime prevention is more crime displacement than true prevention. That is, although it is important to reduce opportunities for criminal victimization wherever it might occur, many crime prevention methods seem to rest on the assumption that predatory crime is inevitable. As a result, they focus on eliminating a specific opportunity for crime instead of treating its underlying causes. Growing numbers of professionals, including the public health community, believe that the prevention of violent and other serious crime by addressing its underlying causes is not only desirable but possible. Promising pilot projects, funded by grant monies, are one way of experimenting with new primary and secondary prevention alternatives to after-the-fact measures.

Both factions in criminal justice—the prevention and control groups—need a specialized tool to help them secure the grant funding they need. Both obviously are trying to address the same general problem from different perspectives. In some cases, each will qualify for different sources of grant funds. It is hoped that this volume will help both groups in implementing their respective solutions.

A number of excellent books are available on the topic of grantsmanship. Some of these are general, whereas others are more specialized. Several of these are listed in Appendix E, "For Further Reading." What makes any particular volume of value to a prospective user is the author's ability to bridge the knowledge it imparts with the personal experience of the reader. And so it is with grantsmanship. If you are a criminal justice practitioner or researcher poring over a generic grantsmanship how-to manual, the "how" as applied to your particular field may not immediately become clear. This book, then, uses specific, hypothetical examples of projects in criminal justice to show exactly how to build a case for funding.

WHO SHOULD BENEFIT FROM THIS BOOK?

Virtually anyone working in a field related to criminal justice or criminology should find this book useful. It is especially intended to help those with little or no experience in grantsmanship. Many criminal justice professionals find themselves in the role of grant seeker, although it may not be part of their formal job duties. The information contained in this book will assist the reader in tackling one of these "other, related duties" known as grantsmanship.

Even the more experienced criminal justice grant seeker may pick up some new pointers from reading this book. This should be true especially of the information on revising and submitting, most of which is grounded in my experience as a grant writer and reviewer. All readers should benefit from the agency contact information, which, in the case of World Wide Web home pages with their many links, will lead them to yet additional sources of information.

Those working in law enforcement should find this book helpful, especially given the recent push to adopt community policing. Although the purists will argue that new funds are not necessary to implement community policing, Congress in recent years has authorized many millions of dollars in grant monies for this purpose. Despite the streamlined simplicity of some of the new federal grant applications, most still require the applicant to substantiate a problem that argues for community policing as the proposed solution. Consequently, law enforcement officials should be able to see that new monies can sometimes help in attempting to undertake new ways of doing business, such as implementing specific programs to promote community policing or taking advantage of advanced criminal justice information systems for tactical and strategic planning.

Through a hydraulic-like effect, the social forces that create crime in the first place put pressure on the rest of the criminal justice system. If a local law enforcement agency makes a sincere attempt to implement community policing, we might expect more arrests. Why? Because the citizens, now trusting of the police in their new roles of community problem solvers, should be more likely to come forward with information about criminal activity in their neighborhood. This is exactly what we should want.

This new flow of information from community residents, however, may translate into more criminal cases for the local prosecutor. In this example, the increase in arrests will spawn a corresponding increase in the prosecutor's workload. The search for help in addressing this problem may lead the prosecutor to a solution that streamlines the management of conventional criminal cases or diverts those less serious cases not requiring the same level of prosecutorial attention as violent and other serious felony cases. Any of these possible solutions to the prosecutor's problem could be tested using grant funds.

It is no secret that in general, victim assistance programs operate on barebones budgets. The reason for this situation is not altogether clear. Perhaps some local governments deem these programs a service they cannot afford. It may also be possible that the strong victim lobby that has resulted in such advances as victims' rights bills has been unable to translate its strength into operating dollars. Whatever the reason, local victim assistance programs may continue to struggle financially. The picture of a victim advocate, weary from long hours trying to meet the demanding needs of clients, extending the workday to complete a grant application is probably more often the rule than the exception. This book, then, may assist victim services workers by increasing their efficiency and success as grant writers.

Nowhere is the hydraulic pressure of criminal cases more apparent than in the courts. As more offenders are identified and arrested, so are they processed from their initial appearance in court to sentencing. In these days when a single change in sentencing laws can give rise to a tsunami of new criminal cases, the courts face a bigger challenge to do more with less. Burgeoning dockets argue for creative solutions. Creative solutions most often require start-up monies to demonstrate their worth. Courts thus have a strong incentive to pursue new ways of doing business. Grants are one way to accomplish this.

Caseloads aside, there are other sound reasons for courts to have an interest in grant funds. Recently, there has been a substantial movement toward reorienting the processing of certain delinquency and criminal cases to *restorative* or *community* justice. This has been true especially in the juvenile justice system. Although these related concepts are no longer new, they now have a sufficient following to capture the attention of federal, state, and private funding organizations. If a court is not willing or able to completely revamp itself around restorative justice, but wants to experiment with the concept, a grant for a pilot project might be an affordable, nonthreatening way to do so. Drug courts are another good example of how the courts have experimented with a unique solution to a particular systemic challenge.

Such creative solutions to the crime problem are not solely the province of government. As more and more emphasis is placed on community-based solutions to crime and social disorder, increasing numbers of nonprofit organizations are undertaking grassroots efforts to improve community life. Neighborhood associations, once largely vehicles for local communication and social gatherings, are now playing a larger role in "taking back the streets." These efforts range from block watch initiatives to conflict mediation and gang reduction strategies. Getting these local efforts off the ground sometimes requires monies for office space, supplies, and transportation, if not salaries. A reference tool such as this book aimed at this audience will, I hope, improve the chances of success for local groups in the competition for limited criminal justice monies.

Academicians in the fields of criminal justice and criminology, especially those without a lot of grant experience, should find this book helpful in their search for research dollars. For years, people within academe and without have almost jokingly referred to the "publish or perish" pressure under which faculty must work. But professors early in their academic careers know this really is not a source of amusement. The tenure and promotion process may have evolved beyond a process wherein scholarly publications are simply tallied. But reality suggests that assistant professors who have not produced a sufficient body of scholarly work in their first 5 or 6 years on the job may well find themselves involuntarily back on the market.

The research that spawns these precious journal articles and books often requires grant dollars. Training in grants and grantsmanship is not normal fare in graduate programs in criminal justice and criminology. A fortunate few young scholars may pick up such skills from research administrators or mentors, but this is more likely to be the exception than the rule. Graduate students who one day intend to assume positions in academic institutions or government agencies should also benefit from the information in this book.

GRANT WRITING AS A SUSPENSE TALE

In the suspense novel, the author draws the reader in with a problem. The protagonist in the novel—the character readers find themselves rooting for—is beset with a problem. This problem is not a hangnail. It is never about what she's going to wear when she goes out that night. The problem in a suspense novel is generally about life or death. Once the protagonist has become drawn into the drama, she stands to lose something precious to her. It could be her life or that of someone about whom she cares deeply.

I have chosen to use the analogy of the suspense novel in illustrating some of the concepts in this book for several reasons. First, the writing of a grant also must be driven by a compelling problem. The problem in a grant proposal cannot be as insignificant as a hangnail. It should be something so important that the readers of the grant proposal or application, like the readers of a fast-paced thriller, do not want to put it down. They want to read on. Ideally, they *must* read on, to the end, where they discover exactly how the character's problem will be solved.

The second reason for using the analogy of the suspense tale is that a grant proposal or application really is a story. Aside from being grounded in a serious problem, the grant proposal, from beginning to end, needs to carry a consistent message to the reader. A grant application, not unlike the suspense tale, is an artful weaving together of problem, people, background, and solution. It needs to keep engaging the reader until the complete case for funding has been made. If the grant writer can carefully construct a story that similarly casts a spell on the funding organization until the end, the chances of securing funding should be much greater.

A third reason for using this device is the reading habits of many criminal justice professionals. For reasons not altogether clear, a number of law enforcement officers enjoy the police novels of such authors as Joseph Wambaugh and William Caunitz. Perhaps it is because the authors were once police officers, and officers reading their books feel they can identify better with writers who actually were "on the job." Or perhaps the readers want to see if the authors really have their details straight. To a lot of observers, a cop reading a novel about cops is analogous to the postal carrier who takes a walk on his or her day off. But whatever the motivation, police novels have among their readers a number of law enforcement officers and other criminal justice professionals.

Much the same can be said of what has become known as the legal thriller. Authors such as Scott Turow and John Grisham have given birth to a genre of suspense novel in which the law or lawyers figure prominently. Just as cops read cop novels, I also suspect that a lot of members of the legal profession enjoy these legal thrillers. Apparently, some criminal justice professionals just can't get enough of their subject matter, whether through labor or leisure.

Regardless of where in criminal justice readers of this book make their contributions, the point is that the development of a case for grant funding, based on a bona fide problem, can be as challenging and entertaining as the suspense novel that professionals read in leisure time. The parallels are there, and the greater extent to which they ring true and thus influence the grant-writing process, the more grantsmanship will be a positive, rewarding experience instead of something to simply dread and avoid.

The last reason for using the suspense novel analogy is to make this book a bit more fun. Let's face it, grantsmanship is fairly dry subject matter. Unlike much other business in criminal justice such as tracking serial killers or exonerating the wrongfully convicted with new DNA evidence, how-to information on writing grants is less than captivating. I have attempted to make this grants primer a little less stuffy by comparing the exercise of grant writing to that of the suspense novel. The analogy is not always perfect; the points of similarity, however, should strike a familiar chord in those readers who also enjoy suspense tales.

One word of caution: Readers should not interpret the lighter tone of this book to mean that I do not take grantsmanship seriously. Grants are an important means of doing the critical, sometimes life-or-death, work in criminal justice. Grant writing often is the only obstacle between a dedicated criminal justice professional and a worthwhile solution to a pressing problem. I assume that readers will approach the writing of grants with the same seriousness of purpose that characterizes their posture toward other professional responsibilities.

GRANT WRITING AS A PARTNERSHIP

The other stylistic device of this book that might convey informality is the use of first person and second person. One reason for this is the awkward construction that results when an author purposely sticks with third person. Generally, the writer is forced (as in this sentence) to use a lot of passive voice. The result is a style that is formal, stilted, and uninteresting. I apologize to all my readers who disagree with my choice. I hope that most readers will appreciate the more conversational style and, consequently, find the entire book more accessible than some of the other works on grantsmanship.

There is a much more compelling reason for such a familiar style. Were I writing a theoretical essay or describing an empirical research study, I would adhere to usual standards of formality, including the extensive use of footnotes, references, and the other common trappings of scholarship. But for me, grantsmanship is different. Preparing grants is not as much grounded in a body of theory and research as it is based on actual experience in having done it. In this sense, grantsmanship is empirical, built on a foundation of countless hours spent writing grants, reviewing applications and proposals, and serving on grant review committees. Consequently, 15 years ago, I couldn't have written this book. But now, having read literally hundreds of grant proposals and applications; having participated in team reviews; having applied for grants successfully and unsuccessfully; and having taught the subject matter to law enforcement planners, drug counselors, victim advocates, and other justice professionals, I believe I now have a feel for how to approach the process. It's that feel that I hope will rub off on the reader.

I am also prepared to argue that grant writing, like many other significant endeavors in contemporary life, is best approached through a partnership. Many of us prefer to go through life with a partner. Many of us are teamed up with partners in the work setting. And so I want you, the reader, to approach grant writing as a partnership—not a partnership in the sense that I'm literally part of your grant-writing team but a partnership in the sense that I'm figuratively peering over your shoulder; reassuring you that success in grantsmanship is possible; offering a few useful suggestions; and maintaining that it can be beneficial, perhaps even fulfilling, if we can later undertake some important work in the field with the much-needed funds.

So in picking up this book, you, the reader, agree to a partnership, an unwritten pact of sorts. My part of the deal is that I will have tried my best to convey to you what you need to succeed in applying for criminal justice grants. In return, all I ask is that you as reader and potential applicant will be open to, if not persuaded by, my advice.

2

Defining the Problem

In general, a problem or a need drives a criminal justice professional's search for monies. A law enforcement agency wants to rid a particular precinct of gang graffiti and other signs of neighborhood decay. A prosecutor's office wants to divert first-time offenders from expensive, labor-intensive formal processing that should be reserved for more serious offenders. A court wants to address an ever-growing backlog of criminal cases. A therapeutic community wants to know if its programming reduces illegal drug use and recidivism among an offender population. A criminologist wants to use survey data to test several hypotheses related to the lifestyle/routine activities approach. All these examples bespeak problems that criminal justice professionals want to solve in one way or another.

The problem that drives a search for criminal justice funding should be compelling. Just as the problem faced by the main character in a suspense novel should be serious enough to hold the readers' interest from the beginning of the book to the last page, the applicant's problem in a grant proposal is expected to catch and hold the interest of funding agencies. The subject matter need not be life or death as it usually is in a suspense tale—but that doesn't hurt, either. Take, for example, the case of an inner-city neighborhood plagued by homicide and serious assault. Wouldn't we expect most people to be more concerned about human lives than issues with less extreme consequences? If an agency in the community submits a funding application for a project designed to reduce the incidence of violent crime, then we should expect it to get more attention from a prospective sponsor than an application centered on something much less threatening.

A PROBLEM FOR WHOM?

The preceding discussion leads us to ask who is affected by the problem. For a criminal justice problem to grab the attention of funding agencies, it needs to affect one or more segments of the human population. It therefore is important for the grant seeker to identify who these people are.

Many subsets of the general population are affected by various crime-related problems. Residents of an urban neighborhood suffering from social disorganization may risk life, limb, and property if that set of problems goes unattended. Recidivism of criminal offenders affects not only the offenders themselves but also the citizens they victimize, the families they fail to financially support, and the community to which they do not positively contribute. Victims of crime suffer from physical, mental, emotional, and financial problems as a result of the crime. Their family members, often referred to as secondary victims, also suffer. The list goes on and on. The point to remember is that people-focused problems are more important than any other type. They are the types of problems that get the attention of funding organizations.

As should be clear from the preceding paragraph, asking who is affected by a criminal justice problem can lead to more than one answer. In the case of criminal victimization, one answer will certainly be the victim. But depending on their specialization in criminal justice, grant applicants might be just as concerned with crime's effect on offenders. Programs incorporating community justice could include both. There is no right or wrong answer to this question. It all depends on the applicant's definition of the problem and who is expected to benefit from the proposed solution. There often are multiple beneficiaries in solving criminal justice problems.

ELEMENTS OF A STRONG PROBLEM

Important problems have profound consequences not only for criminal justice practitioners but also for the community in general. The grant seeker must ask, "What happens if the problem I've identified is not solved?" If the answer suggests that the consequences result in some significant harm to a segment of the community, then the problem is an important one. If, on the other hand, the applicant determines that there will be few or no consequences if the problem goes unsolved, then it should be considered less significant. Table 2.1 lists several problems in criminology and criminal justice and some of the possible consequences they can lead to if unaddressed. The consequences listed are not exhaustive; they are shown merely to illustrate the kind of exercise that grant applicants should go through to gauge the importance of their problem.

Table 2.1   Examples of Criminal Justice Problems and Possible Consequences

Problem	Possible Consequences
Gang activity	Influx of drugs Gang-related violence Loss to gangs of at-risk wanna-bes
Neighborhood decay	Proliferation of crack houses Restriction of activities by citizens Increase in violent crime Drop in property value
Police misconduct	Lack of respect for law enforcement Widespread graft and corruption Threat of reprisals against police
Backlog of court cases	Excessive plea bargaining of cases Necessity of overtime for court employees Denial of speedy justice
Failure to evaluate	Possibility of doing harm to program clients Inability to replicate positive results Perpetuation of mistakes

Criminal justice professionals who are unclear about whether they have a bona fide problem should take the time to go through this exercise, although it may strike some as elementary. A recurring theme in this book is the attention to details that ultimately can help make or break the case for grant funding.

In some cases, such as the problem and consequences listed below, the results suggest that the problems are relatively trivial.

Lack of a computer	Forced to use typewriter
	Must use telephone or mail instead of e-mail
	Can't share computer files with others
	Need more paper for record storage

This example shows that despite some extra cost and inconvenience, business can still go on without the requested item. Does this mean that such items are automatically always trivial and, consequently, unjustifiable in a grant request? Certainly not. It means only that the criminal justice grant seeker must work harder to come up with justifications that will appeal to potential funders.

Many of these weaker problems, then, are actually an absence of tools needed to solve bona fide problems. A police commander's lack of night vision goggles by itself is not a vital problem. These goggles, however, may be an important tool necessary in solving narcotics trafficking taking place at night in the commander's community. In this case, the narcotics trafficking, and how that can spawn violence and otherwise negatively affect the quality of life in the community, constitutes the problem that will interest a sponsor. The night vision goggles are simply a tool or method that enables the applicant to implement the solution to the real problem.

EXAMPLE OF A STRONG PROBLEM

For the sake of illustration, let's examine the case of child homicide. Let's say that we know from an examination of the FBI's Supplementary Homicide Report statistics that many homicide victims are children. Other homicide data from the National Center for Health Statistics confirm this grim picture. The research literature on the subject tells us that there are different types of child homicide. Older children, for example, tend to be killed away from home by strangers using weapons. Their younger counterparts, on the other hand, tend to die at home literally at the hands of their parents and caregivers. Child homicide, then, is not a homogeneous construct; rather, it is a heterogeneous, complex subject deserving of careful dissection by both researchers and practitioners.

We then may want to move our discussion of this problem from the general to the specific. Again, for the sake of illustration, let's pretend that our state and local statistics mirror the evidence available from national sources. We find that a substantial proportion of young children in our community are being killed at home by those who are legally and otherwise responsible for their care. A clear picture of young, innocent children who are senselessly dying begins to emerge from the statistics.

This particular example of a problem offers a unique, compelling element that statistics alone cannot convey. To many people, including those working for funding organizations, children are considered virtually sacrosanct. That is, they are viewed as innocent and vulnerable and, as such, deserving of special consideration and care beyond that which we extend to adults. Consequently, the intentional killing of children by parents and caregivers is seen as an abomination, an affront to civilized society. Such a compelling problem undoubtedly will capture the attention of those reading the grant proposal.

WHAT IS A WEAK PROBLEM?

Just as the life-or-death problem captures the interest of the readers of a suspense thriller, an insignificant problem will bore or annoy them. If the protagonist in our story desperately needs a huge sum of money to get her brother released from his organized criminal captors, this will grab our attention. But if the protagonist simply finds herself without enough money to pay her electric bill, readers won't care in the least—and we can't blame them.

Building on Maslow's now-famous hierarchy of needs, we may deem life-threatening problems as among the most important. Those related to what we might consider creature comforts, then, are likely not to interest most grant-making organizations. These would be at the other extreme of the spectrum of problems. In between lie other problems, many of which deserve the attention of grant-making organizations.

These creature comfort needs that many grant seekers describe in proposals often are related to a lack of resources. In some cases, this might be personnel, computers, or travel funds. In other cases, it might be furniture, supplies, or contractual help. This is *not* what sponsors want to hear. Instead, they want to know about a pressing problem for an identifiable constituent group, for example, people in the applicant's community. The purpose of this section, then, is to help the reader distinguish a legitimate problem worthy of prospective sponsors' attention from one they will ignore.

The weak problem in criminal justice can go unattended, and no one will be significantly affected. For example, if a nonprofit violence prevention organization does not have a brochure to distribute, will any segment of the human population suffer in large part? Probably not. If this organization were trying to secure grant funds for the printing of such a brochure, their problem—that people did not know about them and their work—might pale in comparison with other problems related to violence in the community. Does this mean that the brochures are not fundable? Certainly not. It just means that across the spectrum of criminal justice problems, the lack of a brochure may not figure among the most pressing. More likely, the brochure is a tool for helping the applicant solve a far more serious problem such as domestic violence.

EXAMPLE OF A WEAK PROBLEM

Let's imagine that we have a victim advocate who works in a victim assistance program. Her agency is a nonprofit organization that depends largely on donations, fund-raising drives, and the local United Way for funding. As a result, by usual standards, the advocate must carry out her victim advocacy with a minimum of material resources.

She maintains paper files on all her clients. This victim services program cannot afford a personal computer for her to maintain agency records. As a result, she spends an inordinate time manually making entries about court appearances, referrals to social services agencies, the confinement status of her clients' victimizers, and a host of other necessary transactions. Such manual entry and subsequent retrieval consume time that she could be spending on serving the needs of her victim clients.

Consequently, she applies for a grant from a local community foundation. She argues in her problem statement that she lacks a computer. A computer, she argues, is the only major piece of equipment her office lacks, because she already has a fax machine and photocopier. She further buttresses her case by stating that every other victim assistance program with which she is familiar has a personal computer.

The community foundation denies her request. In their written response, foundation staff tell her that although they are sensitive to the value of computers in the contemporary workplace, they do not feel her lack of a computer could be linked to the segment of the population they wanted to serve, in this instance, victims of serious crime.

Where did our advocate go wrong? Her real problem was not that she lacked a personal computer. Instead, what she should have emphasized is that many needs of her victim clients were going unattended because of the time and effort she had to spend on manual record keeping. It was the victims of crime and their important needs that the community foundation cared most about. Couching the problem in relation to the victims would have captured the foundation's attention. Instead, our advocate inadvertently made herself and the inconvenience of not having a computer the focus and, thereby, lost the interest of a potential sponsor. If this were to really happen, it would be especially distressing, inasmuch as the victim advocate faced a serious problem in which many prospective sponsors would be interested.

IN WHAT PROBLEMS ARE SPONSORS INTERESTED?

Federal agencies often have their problems defined for them by Congress. For example, state agencies administering the Edward Byrne Memorial State and Local Law Enforcement Assistance Program (see list in Appendix B) have more than 20 program categories from which to choose in determining the types of problems they want to address with these funds. These categories were determined by Congress in the authorizing legislation. So the Bureau of Justice Assistance, the federal agency administering the Byrne program, has limited discretion in how it determines the funding structures it passes on to the state administering agencies (SAAs). The good news for applicants, however, is that in most criminal justice formula grants programs, there is a substantial amount of latitude in the types of criminal justice problems that fit within the guidelines.

The same is true for the other federal and state agencies. For example, the state agencies responsible for administering the STOP Violence Against Women Grants Program at the state level also have certain guidelines that specify applicant eligibility and purpose areas. The Office of Juvenile Justice and Delinquency Prevention, which also has formula grants programs administered by the states, is yet another example. But within the constraints imposed by the authorizing legislation, there remains a great deal of latitude to undertake meaningful, innovative programming in criminal and juvenile justice. Only careful examination of application materials will tell applicants the fit between their problems and the possible sources of money for solutions.

Private foundations and corporations, on the other hand, have boards that determine their funding emphases. Often, these emphases relate to the interests of those who endowed the foundation. Most private foundations make clear their areas of interest in the reference works on foundations, on their World Wide Web home pages, and elsewhere. Once again, the prospective applicant should not be discouraged; the areas of interest of both governmental organizations and private foundations are often broad, permitting creative applicants to propose innovative programming or research that solves their particular problem.

EXAMPLE 2A: MAKING THE CASE FOR A COMMUNITY POLICING PROGRAM

Community policing has been around long enough now that it is not simply a buzzword. Many law enforcement agencies around the country have institutionalized it as the principal means of policing. Many other departments are struggling with exactly what community policing is or should be. Still, because of the general popularity of the concept, coupled with the federal monies directed toward its implementation, there will continue to be a lot of interest in it throughout the coming years.

Community policing as the backbone of a problem statement is not as easy a sell as one might think. As mentioned earlier, a number of purists believe that community policing requires philosophical and organizational change more than it does programmatic monies. If we accept this view, it will be more difficult, but perhaps not impossible, to argue for funds to facilitate its implementation.

We need, then, to demonstrate a problem for which community policing is an appropriate solution. Crime is an obvious choice. This means that we need to paint a detailed statistical picture of violent and property crime in the community. Our picture could also include public order offenses that may be indirectly related to more serious crime and the overall quality of life. What are the trends showing? Is the crime rate going up? If it isn't going up in general, is it rising within certain segments of the community? How is the problem worsening in a way that will get the attention of those reading the grant proposal?

A community suffering from crime and social decay has statistics other than crime data it can use to construct an effective problem statement. For example, how many times has the city been called on to mow the grass of property owners who had neglected their responsibilities? How many complaints have been lodged about junk automobiles in yards and vacant lots? How often has graffiti been reported? Where have these instances occurred? If we were to pinpoint these locations on a city map, they may well form a pattern. That pattern, in turn, can show an area of the city that is in a state of neglect. It could be argued that if this trend isn't reversed, the situation will worsen.

What do the above statistics mean relative to a serious problem that will get the attention of funding organizations? Are residents fleeing to the suburbs because of the decline of the neighborhood? Have property values decreased as a result? Do citizens in the community feel less safe than they did 5 years ago? Three years ago? The imaginative grant seeker should be able to identify a number of nontraditional ways of measuring the problems in the community that help make the case for community policing. These statistics will support the case that a real problem does exist.

EXAMPLE 2B: MAKING THE CASE FOR A PROSECUTOR'S DIVERSION PROGRAM

Despite their general reputation as hard-nosed, get-tough professionals, prosecutors sometimes conclude that traditional criminal case processing may not always be the best way or the only way to serve the ends of justice. Many realize that first-time minor offenders can be better served by programming that is less punitive and more rehabilitative.

Diversion, one alternative to traditional processing, gives first-time nonviolent offenders a chance to avoid immediate prosecution if they are willing to abide by certain conditions for a specified period. If the diverted offender meets the conditions of his or her diversion without new offenses or infractions of the rules, the pending charges will be dismissed. Diversion has been used effectively for many years now, and it can save a prosecutor scarce resources needed for more serious criminal cases.

A prosecutor wanting to start a diversion unit can make a strong case in the problem statement in a couple of ways. One way is to show the numbers of criminal cases coming into the office. Most often, a prosecutor's cases are a function of charges originally filed by local law enforcement. In the problem statement, then, the prosecutor wants to show how many cases are being referred by law enforcement as well as by other sources of referral.

More persuasive than simply the number of criminal cases being referred is an increasing trend. Here, a line graph of the number of cases increasing through time is an effective means of showing the prosecutor's worsening caseload. This could be supplemented by showing the caseload of individual prosecutors in the office, perhaps as compared with regional or national standards, demonstrating unreasonable workload demands on staff.

This is only the beginning of the case the prosecutor can make. How many of those referred cases result in hours spent with the grand jury seeking indictments? How many hours of case preparation are needed for cases that ultimately get plea bargained? The number of hours will be even greater for cases going to trial.

The prosecutor may also choose to focus on the impact these more minor cases have for the office's success in more serious cases. Bogged down by having to process large numbers of first-time nonviolent felons, the prosecutor may have insufficient resources to devote to the violent and other serious felons the community fears the most.

When the prosecutor's problem statement is completed, there should be no doubt in the mind of those reading the grant proposal that the problem is grave enough to warrant serious attention. The problem is grounded not only in wasted time that prosecutors spend on these cases but also in the missed opportunity to give minor offenders an important second chance. If successfully made, the case for funding will more than adequately demonstrate that the consequences of the problem are too severe to go unattended.

EXAMPLE 2C: MAKING THE CASE
FOR A RESTORATIVE JUSTICE PROJECT

Why do we want to experiment with this concept called restorative justice? Because we like to be trendy? No. Because there is federal funding set aside for such projects? No. Instead, our rationale in undertaking an experiment in restorative justice should be grounded in problems with the conventional way we administer criminal or juvenile justice. What might some of the problems be?

In traditional processing of criminal cases, the victim many times is left dissatisfied. Why? Often, offenders are processed by the criminal justice system in such a way as to give little or no accounting to the victim. In some cases, no amount of jail or prison time for the defendant is necessarily going to help victims back to the state they enjoyed prior to the commission of the offense. Criminal justice processing cannot go back in time and make the crime go away, but in many cases, it could determine the ways in which the victim might be physically, financially, psychologically, emotionally, and otherwise restored. When the system fails to attend to these needs, it stands accused of victimizing the victim a second time.

For the offender, traditional processing is still largely retributive, despite the trend toward graduated sanctions and other more recent correctional innovations. What does a criminal offender really need? If we believe that the offender was never "habilitated" in the first place, then assisting this person in becoming a law-abiding, responsible, contributing member of society might be a good place to begin. Part of that process revolves around making offenders aware of the implications of their actions in the current offense and helping them develop insights into the consequences their actions have for the victim and for society in general. Recidivism and continued poor social adjustment may be the result of inattention to these issues.

Inasmuch as "the people" are represented by the prosecutor in criminal cases, they too have an interest in the administration of justice. Is society as retributive as recent legislation would have us believe? Or would the majority of us rather see convicted offenders give something back to the community they've just victimized? Restorative justice permits the community to heal in the wake of a crime by making its requirements known and consequently giving offenders the opportunity to restore a sense of equity and safety that is violated when a crime is committed. A community held captive by the fear of crime is not truly part of a free society.

So how do we substantiate these problems for which restorative justice is the solution? There are a number of possibilities. We might consider conducting a survey of victims, offenders, and others participating in traditional processing in an effort to assess their satisfaction with case outcomes. A corresponding survey of the general citizenry might yield not only their dissatisfaction with the administration of justice but also their suggestions for more satisfactory outcomes. Citizens may reveal that they are afraid of crime and criminals. They may not feel free to walk about in their neighborhood. It may then be a restored sense of safety and security that they require from a restorative justice process. We might also appeal to the research literature to demonstrate that traditional processing tends to be followed by offender recidivism, high incarceration costs, and anger and frustration of victims. In assessing community attitudes, we may find that citizens are actually supportive of measures that help restore victims, offenders, and the community as a whole.

EXAMPLE 2D: MAKING THE CASE
FOR A COMMUNITY-BASED
CORRECTIONAL FACILITY PROJECT

In our hypothetical corrections example, our community-based correctional facility (CBCF) is having a problem with the recidivism of its clients. The corrections system, by definition, is designed through one means or another to turn around the lives of those who have broken the law. But we can't take anything for granted; we have to make a strong, statistically based case for this problem, as we would with any other criminal justice problem.

A follow-up evaluation of offender outcomes will show the extent to which our CBCF is or is not successful in rehabilitating clients. In this case, we might provide outcome data for those sentenced to prison, intensive supervision probation, electronic monitoring, and other correctional alternatives. What should emerge is that our CBCF, designed to provide a less restrictive and more rehabilitative means of dealing with convicted offenders, shows little improvement over the other alternatives in client outcomes. That is, many of the clients assigned to this alternative end up violating by way of failed drug tests.

So why not just shut down the program and sentence these offenders to prison? A major point in finding alternatives in the first place was to reduce the tremendous cost represented by confinement in a state penal institution. We have already addressed this cost issue with the use of a CBCF. We now want to solve a different, albeit related problem, that of decreasing the recidivism of CBCF residents.

DOCUMENTING THE PROBLEM

It's a good idea to make sponsors aware of previous attempts to address the problem at hand. Seldom are we the first to grapple with the problem we've identified. It is incumbent upon us, then, to describe what we found in the scholarly and professional literature. How pervasive is the problem? How is the problem in our jurisdiction similar to or different from that in other areas?

It is one thing to know a problem exists. It is quite another to make a convincing case that it does. Funding organizations are persuaded more by numbers and other hard evidence than by the mere assertion that the problem exists. This does not imply that the funding organization is distrustful of the applicant's motives for seeking funding. Most funding organizations receive applications or proposals from large numbers of applicants. They therefore must put their grant dollars toward the most pressing of problems or those most persuasively argued. The evidence the applicant brings to bear tells them which problems are most urgent and consequently in need of their limited funding.

The applicant, therefore, should paint a statistical picture of the problem. How serious is the problem? Is it getting worse through time? How does the affected jurisdiction compare with other similar jurisdictions? What segment of the population is affected most by the problem? These and other questions can be answered with appropriate statistics.

SOURCES OF STATISTICS

Inasmuch as we've just argued for a statistical picture of the problem in the problem statement, we need to know where a grant seeker in criminology or criminal justice can find some of these numbers. The following list of information sources is not exhaustive. These are among the first places a grant seeker should consult to find relevant statistical data.

As with most professional contacts, such inquiries will in many cases lead to yet other useful sources. This is true no matter how the contact is made. In searching the World Wide Web for statistical sources, we should always check the home page's "Links." These often direct the user to other relevant sources of statistics. When searching for statistical and other relevant information to support a problem statement, we should always ask the source for yet other sources. In time, we will eventually begin turning up the same sources already identified. This is a sign that we probably have covered most, if not all, of the sources that can help us.

Sourcebook of Criminal Justice Statistics

This valuable sourcebook, a compilation of criminal justice statistics on a wide variety of topics, is a project of the School of Criminal Justice at the University of Albany, State University of New York, sponsored by the federal Bureau of Justice Statistics. Because it has been produced for more than two decades, users can examine trends in many of these data—a benefit for grant seekers. The volume is arranged according to five major topical areas:

1. Characteristics of the criminal justice systems
2. Public attitudes toward crime and criminal justice–related topics
3. Nature and distribution of known offenses
4. Judicial processing of defendants
5. Persons under correctional supervision

The sourcebook should be available in most public and university libraries. It is also available on the Internet at http://www.albany.edu/sourcebook/. The on-line version enables users to search for topics using key words and to download files to their computers.

National Criminal Justice Reference Service

The National Criminal Justice Reference Service (NCJRS) is considered the reference library for the U.S. Department of Justice and its many funding arms and agencies. As such, it is the source for countless documents and statistics that the criminal justice grant seeker may need. In some cases, the NCJRS can fax documents to the requestor; in other cases, staff may mail hard copy of the document. The NCJRS may also refer the requestor to other, more appropriate sources for statistics.

One especially useful feature is the NCJRS Abstracts Database. This resource contains summaries of more than 140,000 reports, journal articles, and monographs related to crime and criminal justice. The full citation is listed in case the user needs to track down the original source document.

The NCJRS can be contacted at

National Criminal Justice Reference Service
2277 Research Blvd.
Rockville, MD 20850
Phone: (800) 851-3420 or (301) 519-5500
E-mail: askncjrs@aspensys.com
WWW: http://www.ncjrs.org/

Bureau of Justice Statistics

The Bureau of Justice Statistics (BJS) is one of several arms of the Office of Justice Programs in the U.S. Department of Justice. For the grant seeker in criminology or criminal justice, the bureau should be considered an important source for statistical data, especially those at the national level. The BJS collects, analyzes, publishes, and disseminates information on crime, criminal offenders, victims of crime, and the operation of justice systems at all levels of government.

The BJS can be contacted at

Bureau of Justice Statistics
810 Seventh Street, NW
Washington, DC 20531
Phone: (202) 307-0765
E-mail: askbjs@ojp.usdoj.gov
WWW: http://www.ojp.usdoj.gov/bjs

National Center for State Courts

The National Center for State Courts (NCSC) is an independent, nonprofit organization dedicated to the improvement of justice. It has a long track record of conducting studies related to courts and the administration of criminal justice. For the applicant wishing to pursue a court-related project, a visit to the home page of the NCSC may prove more than worthwhile. The NCSC provides leadership and service to the state courts by undertaking the following activities:

- Developing policies to enhance state courts
- Advancing state courts' interests within the federal government
- Fostering state court adaptation to future changes
- Securing sufficient resources for state courts
- Strengthening state court leadership
- Facilitating state court collaboration
- Providing a model for organizational administration

The NCSC can be contacted at

National Center for State Courts
300 Newport Avenue
Williamsburg, VA 23185
Phone: (757) 253-2000
Fax: (757) 220-0449
WWW: http://www.ncsc.dni.us/

National Center for Policy Analysis

The National Center for Policy Analysis (NCPA) approaches policy issues from a free-enterprise view. To that end, it strives for creative solutions that are grounded in the private, rather than the public, sector. The NCPA's major areas of interest include tax policy, health care policy, criminal justice, Social Security and Medicare, environment, and welfare reform.

The types of information the NCPA maintains holdings on include

- Statistics and forecasts
- Juvenile crime
- Causes and prevention
- Criminals
- Police policies
- Punishment
- Criminal justice system
- Privatizing law enforcement and justice
- Self-defense and gun control

The NCPA can be contacted at

National Center for Policy Analysis
727 15th Street, NW, 5th Floor
Washington, DC 20005
Phone: (202) 628-6671
Fax: (202) 628-6474
WWW: http://www.public-policy.org/~ncpa/pi/crime/crime.html

National Clearinghouse on Child Abuse and Neglect

The National Clearinghouse on Child Abuse and Neglect (NCCAN) is exactly what the title implies. Anyone preparing a grant proposal related to these issues should contact this organization for data, reports, and other relevant information.

The NCCAN can be contacted at

National Clearinghouse on Child Abuse and Neglect
P.O. Box 1182
Washington, DC 20013-1182
Phone: (800) 394-3366 or (703) 385-7565
Fax: (703) 385-3206
E-mail: nccanch@calib.com
WWW: http://www.calib.com/nccanch/

Center for the Study and Prevention of Violence

The Center for the Study and Prevention of Violence is housed at the University of Colorado at Boulder. Among its purposes is the dissemination of knowledge to those in the violence prevention field. Of particular interest to the grant seeker is the Information House, the core of the center that collects, maintains, retrieves, and disseminates literature and statistics about violence. Its home page is well worth the visit.

The center may be contacted at

> Center for the Study and Prevention of Violence
> Institute of Behavioral Science
> University of Colorado at Boulder
> Campus Box 442
> Boulder, CO 80309-0442
> Phone: (303) 492-8465
> Fax: (303) 443-3297
> WWW: http://www.colorado.edu/cspv/

National Center for Juvenile Justice

As the research division of the National Council of Juvenile and Family Court Judges, the National Center for Juvenile Justice (NCJJ) should be considered by criminal justice grant seekers as one of the first stops for statistics, especially those relating to juvenile justice, delinquency, and unruliness. The NCJJ maintains an active research program, so many of the data they archive are their own.

Included in its extensive holdings are

- National Juvenile Court Data Archive
- Technical Assistance Resource Center
- Family Court Resource Center
- Statistics and Systems Development Resource Center
- Automated Juvenile Law Archive
- Juvenile Probation Officer Initiative Database

The NCJJ can be contacted at

> National Center for Juvenile Justice
> 710 Fifth Avenue, Suite 3000
> Pittsburgh, PA 15219-3000
> Phone: (412) 227-6950
> Fax: (412) 227-6955
> E-mail: ncjj2@nauticom.net
> WWW: http://www.ncjj.org

Inter-University Consortium on Political and Social Science

The Inter-University Consortium on Political and Social Research (ICPSR) includes the National Archive of Criminal Justice Data (NACJD). The NACJD's purpose is to facilitate and encourage research in the field of criminal justice through the preservation and sharing of data resources and the provision of specialized training in quantitative analysis of crime and justice data.

Persons affiliated with institutions that are members of ICPSR may borrow most data sets free of charge. Others will be nominally charged for the data they request. Data can be downloaded from ICPSR to the requestor's computer. The grant seeker in need of crime-related data should consult ICPSR's catalog, which has an extensive list of crime- and justice-related studies.

The ICPSR can be contacted at

> Inter-University Consortium on Political and Social Science
> The University of Michigan
> Institute for Social Research
> P.O. Box 1248
> Ann Arbor, MI 48106-1248
>
> 426 Thompson Street
> Ann Arbor, MI 48104-2321
> Phone: (313) 764-2570
> Fax: (313) 764-8041
> E-mail: netmail@icpsr.umich.edu
> WWW: http://www.icpsr.umich.edu

SOURCES OF STATE STATISTICS

State Administering Agencies

Most states and territories have SAAs, many of which also serve as state criminal justice planning agencies. These agencies typically perform a number of functions including grants administration, research and evaluation, and policy development. Many have research and evaluation data that would be helpful to grant seekers (see Appendix B). Some of these have World Wide Web home pages that the grant seeker may want to visit.

Statistical Analysis Centers

Statistical analysis centers (SACs), many of which are located within the SAAs mentioned above, serve states and territories by collecting, storing, retrieving, and disseminating a variety of statistics related to crime and criminal justice. The SACs are subdivisions within state government that use operational, management, and research information from all components of the criminal justice system to conduct research on statewide and systemwide policy issues. They receive financial support from the Bureau of Justice Statistics to carry out their mission. There are SACs in most states and territories. The SACs can be found in a variety of state agencies, including state police agencies, offices of attorneys general, departments of corrections, and SAAs.

The topics on which the grant seeker can get SAC data are unlimited. Although not all SACs collect statistics on every conceivable subject in the field, their very nature suggests that they are one of the first places someone writing a problem statement should stop. Their areas of interest are detailed in *Criminal Justice Issues in the States,* an annual compilation of SAC research initiatives published by the Justice Research and Statistics Association. A complete list of SACs can be found in Appendix A.

Supreme Courts

State supreme courts generally are good sources of judicial and other court statistics. If criminal justice grant seekers want to ground their problem in the flow of court cases, the supreme court might be able to provide data on arraignments, trials, negotiated cases, and dispositions.

Offices of Attorneys General

The statistics offered by these offices will vary from state to state. In some cases, the offices will house the SACs mentioned above. In other cases, they will not, but they still may maintain databases that criminal justice professionals can use to document state or local problems. Like most state agencies, attorneys general now have World Wide Web home pages that highlight what the agencies have to offer.

Departments of Correction

Departments of correction are responsible for maintaining state correctional facilities for convicted felons. Their research sections generally maintain data not only on the flow of offenders but also on inmate population projections, recidivism, drug use, prison gang activity, and a host of other issues. The grant seeker pursuing a corrections-related problem would be remiss not to contact the state corrections agency to discover what relevant data are available.

Departments of Health

These departments are a source that grant seekers in criminal justice and criminology may overlook. For those interested in such issues as homicide or suicide, for example, state departments of health can provide a variety of vital statistics, many of which derive from death certificate data. These data typically include, but are not necessarily limited to, date, time, place, and cause of death. Health departments may also have data on intentional injuries, illegal drug use, and other issues of interest to criminal justice researchers and practitioners.

SOURCES OF LOCAL STATISTICS

Law Enforcement Agencies

Local law enforcement agencies often keep statistics that prove useful to the criminal justice grant seeker. For example, many law enforcement agencies participate in the FBI's Uniform Crime Reporting program. Its statistics include the number of persons arrested and the number of offenses reported.

As more law enforcement agencies are adopting the National Incident-Based Reporting System (NIBRS) and similar incident-based systems, the grant seeker will be able to secure more crime data. These data, in turn, should make it easier for grant applicants to describe local crime problems in greater detail, which should strengthen their cases for funding.

With the advent of community policing, law enforcement agencies are beginning to expand the types of data they routinely collect. Some community policing officers hold neighborhood meetings at which residents' concerns are aired. The minutes or notes from such meetings are data and, as such, hold the promise of being able to document local problems. In some communities, community policing officers distribute cards on which comments or concerns can be recorded. These in turn are mailed back to the law enforcement agency. Such nontraditional forms of data can be extremely useful for the grant seeker who is trying to document a local problem.

Many sheriff's offices are also responsible for maintaining jails. In such cases, they may have data on inmate drug use, attempted and completed inmate suicides, attempted and completed escapes, length of stay in jail awaiting trial, and other jail-related issues. In some instances, these data may be electronically retrievable.

Local Courts

Courts in counties and other local subdivisions may collect and report data on criminal cases. This is especially true if the court has an automated case management system. Although transactional data are laborious to collect manually, local courts have detailed information on criminal cases including arraignment, pretrial hearings, plea negotiations, trials, sentencing, and probation, as well as case and other offender-specific data. These data are especially useful for establishing court-related caseload problems. They also can be used for research and evaluation on criminal case outcomes and changes in sentencing laws.

3

Questions to Ask Before Starting

Most grantsmanship how-to manuals keep the elements of the grant proposal together. But before formally starting the grant-writing process, you should pose a number of questions to yourself. The following list is not exhaustive; the intention is to keep the criminal justice grant seeker from minimizing the job ahead. As you read the following questions and explanations, yet other questions may arise. That's good. It shows you're dissecting the grant preparation process into its constituent parts. It also shows you're anticipating grantsmanship problems in the beginning when they can be corrected. In doing so, you begin to then think about what all needs to be done, who will do it, when it has to be done, and other such important questions.

Nor are the following questions necessarily profound. You might think that most or all of them are so commonsensical that they don't warrant a mention. Nevertheless, grant applicants invariably fail to take into consideration all the challenges they face as they search for a solution to their problem. Asking and answering these questions should limit wasted time and effort.

Do you have the ability to write a grant proposal?

As you will see throughout this book, preparing a grant proposal involves a lot of writing. After all, this is the medium through which you communicate your problem and proposed solution to potential funding sources. This will be true even if one day everyone submits funding requests electronically via the Internet. The proposals will still have to be communicated by way of the written word.

So you ask yourself if you can communicate your problem, solution, and financial need in writing. Your ability to undertake the proposed project may be judged in part on the way you have related it to the funding organization. Writing the proposal in clear, understandable prose is extremely important. If the grant-making agency can't understand your explanation of the problem, it is unlikely that it will be interested in funding your proposed solution.

No matter how much how-to material is available, some applicants for criminal justice grants simply will not be able to successfully undertake the job. In such a case, the applicant should find a strong writer who can articulate the case for funding. Ideally, this will be a colleague or perhaps a volunteer. In some instances, the applicant may have to enlist the services of a paid grant writer to perform this task. Either way, the result must be a well-stated case for funding an innovative solution to a pressing problem.

Do you have the time to write a grant proposal?

Most professionals in criminal justice and criminology who write grant applications and proposals have other full-time responsibilities. The law enforcement officer who is assigned the task of writing the drug elimination grant application may also be the department's full-time crime prevention officer. The individual who assumes the job of writing a drug court grant may be the court administrator, whose job already encompasses human resources, docket management, and a host of other responsibilities. The professor of criminology or criminal justice juggles teaching responsibilities, research, committee work, and academic writing commitments. Usually, only large organizations can afford to have on the payroll staff members whose sole responsibility is to prepare and administer grants. That being the case, you as grant seeker must ask yourself if you have the flexibility in your professional schedule to write a grant proposal. If not, are you willing or able to devote your personal time to preparing a grant application? And if you're willing to devote your own time, are you prohibited from doing so by union contracts or other similar restrictions?

As will become clear by the end of this book, grant writing is a rather involved process of thinking, planning, drafting, calculating, researching, and other time-consuming activities. If your schedule will not permit you to devote the time necessary to do it right, perhaps you should either not attempt it yourself or try to identify others who do have the time in their schedules. Concern about time may lead to a team approach, one in which several individuals tackle the job of writing the proposal. This makes even more sense when the team members have unique, respective strengths they can bring to the grant-writing process.

Time for preparing a grant application or proposal can also be a function of when you hear about a funding opportunity. For example, many of the grant solicitations issued by federal grant-making agencies allow only a few weeks to apply before the deadline. The time you have to prepare such an application, then, often is constrained somewhat by the sponsor. In a case such as this, you have to ask yourself if you really have enough time to apply. There are problems to document, project activities to detail, library research to conduct, budgets to calculate, and letters of participation to solicit, all within a few weeks. You must ask yourself if all this is going to be possible, given everything else you have to do.

Do you have available the human resources to write a grant proposal?

Perhaps too often, a single person attempts to tackle the job of writing a criminal justice grant. Sometimes, this happens because of an assignment from a superior. The inexperienced grant seeker should not try to do everything. Few of us are expert in all phases of grant preparation. As mentioned above, trading on the strengths of others generally increases the applicant's chances for success.

In the introduction, I talked about the notion of partnership. Partnership is not just some trendy buzzword that is destined to turn into a cliché. Rather, partnership conveys the notion that a team of people, each member strong or expert in his or her own right, can do a better job than any one of the constituent members. This should make perfect sense to all of us.

If you as applicant do not have sufficient skills to single-handedly prepare a grant proposal, can you identify others to help you? This will include, but not necessarily be limited to, researchers, fiscal specialists, writers, support staff, and others. Although it is true that too many cooks can spoil the proverbial broth, a well-coordinated team of talented chefs should be capable of putting together an exquisite meal. Like the persons who will be eating that meal, those at the funding organization who read your proposal should come away from the experience well satisfied.

Can you conduct the necessary research for the proposal?

A project that ultimately hopes to implement community policing as a solution for neighborhood violence and disorder should be based on true principles of community policing. If you are assigned to prepare such an application or proposal, do you know how to find the materials you need? Many of us seldom set foot in a library, let alone know how to avail ourselves of its many resources. Others have never tried to find relevant materials through the Internet and World Wide Web. Do you know how to ground your proposal in the literature of the field? Sometimes, direct service projects get funded without a literature review. But as I will argue throughout this book, the more the problem and its solution are grounded in data and certified knowledge, the greater the chances are that the project in question will be an effective solution to the problem.

For a research or an evaluation project, the library work is never optional. There are those of us, however, who have gotten out of the habit of doing background research. If you can't or won't do the necessary research, do you have a member of your team who can and will?

What are the consequences of not getting the grant?

This is one of the first questions to ask in deciding whether to pursue grant funding. A common practice of applicants—criminal justice or otherwise—is to apply for grants simply because the funds are available and the agency is eligible. This practice will not stop, but it violates the fundamental premise of this book, that is, a real problem—an important one—should drive the entire grant-seeking process.

If the answer to the above question is that little or nothing will happen if you don't get grant funds, then you probably don't really need the grant. You may not even have a bona fide problem. Sure, a lot of agencies apply for the funds just to get their "fair share." But there's a lot of work to be done in administering the grant if you get it. If you don't have a real problem that needs to be solved, will the grant funds be worth the work you will have to do later?

Is there another way of solving this problem?

Not all criminal justice problems require grants to implement the solution. If a law enforcement agency, for example, needs specialized equipment, it may not be able to find an appropriate source of grant funds. The agency may also conclude that it is easier to get the needed funds from a local service organization than it is to put together a grant proposal. Grants are an important vehicle for solving criminal justice problems, but they are not the only one.

Do you know where to look for a grant?

It's one thing to know you need grant money to solve a problem; it's a different challenge to identify the possible funding sources. One of the purposes of this book is to help steer you toward sources of information and funds. But a serious search for monies to address your problem should not stop with the suggestions listed here. Even when you use contemporary devices such as the Internet to search for grant opportunities, it can be a rather time-consuming task, especially for the beginner.

Do you have someone to help paint the statistical picture of your problem?

As we saw in Chapter 2, your problem must be buttressed with statistics. Are you comfortable working with various statistics? Do you know how to draw logical inferences from the data you've collected for your problem statement? If you cannot do this yourself, have you identified someone who can and will?

Statistical data cannot be presented haphazardly. Data are used often enough in contemporary documents that readers' expectations are high, including those of funding organizations. In addition to presenting statistical data accurately, many reviewers have come to expect graphically pleasing presentations. If you aren't comfortable with making the appropriate inferences about the statistical data that support your problem, have you identified someone who is?

Do you have someone to help you with the budget?

Just as some professionals have an aversion to computers or writing, others suffer from anxiety about numbers. Those with such anxiety may not have the aptitude to generate a respectable budget.

The numbers in the budget section of an application or proposal must be correct. They must also reflect certain administrative rules, union contracts, and other requirements with which the inexperienced grant writer may not be familiar. This can be a rather complicated project by itself. It's not impossible, but it's also an activity that may require some special assistance.

Do you have access to quality word processing equipment?

Many of us take for granted the personal computers on our desks, connected to state-of-the-art laser printers, scanners, and other such devices that give us access to the World Wide Web and other modern-day conveniences. In doing so, we inadvertently are arrogant. Many small criminal justice agencies do not have updated equipment on which to prepare a quality grant proposal. Some professionals are forced to use outdated computers and software. Others are still using typewriters. These are facts of life in criminal justice agencies with limited resources.

When grant reviewers read proposals and applications, they cannot help but be impressed by a clean, neat, professionally prepared document. On the contrary, grant proposals that are less than neat, perhaps with strikeovers, blurry characters, archaic fonts, poorly constructed tables, or other distractions, may subconsciously set a negative tone for the grant reviewers. Because you want to do everything you possibly can to enhance your chances of getting funded, will you be able to prepare a professional-looking document that will impress the reviewers?

If you don't have this equipment, some public libraries have computers that patrons can use. There are also businesses that make available computer equipment often at an hourly rate. Everything being equal, appearance counts for something in the competition for grant money. It therefore is important that the grant seeker somehow gain access to the equipment necessary to produce a quality application or proposal.

What is your agency's grant history?

An organization's grant history, much like an individual's credit history, can follow the organization for some time. Some organizations have established impressive histories of securing prestigious grants from federal agencies and private foundations. Such a history gives evidence to potential funding entities that the applicant organization will undertake the proposed project in a responsible manner. This type of history builds on itself, so that with each awarded and successfully administered grant, the applicant organization keeps improving its record and future chances of funding.

If, on the other hand, your agency has performed poorly on previous grants, this may become known to those from whom you seek funding. Some grant applications ask for prior grant history. Should an examination of that history show problems with the administration of prior grants, your chances of getting the current grant award may be hurt. Examples of such problems are failure to submit required fiscal or programmatic reports, questionable audit findings, having a project fold because of mismanagement, and other difficulties linked to poor grant administration.

The point in asking the above questions is not to discourage you, the criminal justice grant applicant. To the contrary, they are designed to help you prepare well in advance for the job ahead. Doing so will consequently improve your chances of success.

4

Methods
Describing the Solution

Whether the problem is a research question or an issue of interest to practitioners, it begs for a solution. That is, after all, the point of most grant proposals. What is the applicant going to do to address the problem? This portion of the grant proposal or application, often referred to as the methods section, tells the sponsor what the applicant proposes as a solution to the problem.

Sponsors expect detail when reading the description of the solution in an application or proposal. They want to know that the applicant is not attempting to reinvent a broken wheel. They want to know that the innovation being proposed shows some promise and is not just a repackaging of an old, stale idea. It therefore is the obligation of the applicant to cover what has been done to date. This coverage should include evaluations of similar solutions. What has the applicant learned from these evaluations that will make the proposed solution stronger and more promising?

QUESTIONS TO ANSWER IN THE METHODS SECTION

The methods section of a grant application should always answer several questions. These questions are similar to the questions that journalists answer as they prepare a story for broadcast or print. We will limit the questions, however, to *who, what, where, when,* and *how.* The *why* question should have already been thoroughly answered in the problem statement.

Who

Any project necessitating grant funding will have one or more persons performing the work. As we discuss the details of how our proposed solution is going to solve the problem outlined in the problem statement, we need to make explicit their respective roles. What will the staff, consultants, and contractual help be doing in the way of project activities? How do people, other than the target population, fit into the project?

For example, let's say we're researchers who intend to undertake an empirical test of the lifestyle/routine activities approach in criminology. Someone, presumably the principal investigator or project director, will be in charge of our research project. Our project also implies that someone will collect, enter, clean, analyze, and interpret the data used to test this theory. There even may be a statistical consultant to advise on complicated data analyses.

At this point in the proposal, we do not need to go into the qualifications of those performing these respective roles. But the methods section should be written in such a way as to suggest the various roles that people will play in carrying out the project's activities. Staff qualifications, which are also important, will be covered in Chapter 7 on capabilities.

What

The answer to this is the crux of the methods section. The whole point of this section is to demonstrate to the funding organization what we intend to do to solve the problem. They need to know exactly what set of project activities we'll undertake if we get the grant.

As mentioned above, more, rather than fewer, details will serve our interests. Again, not all those working for funding organizations are specialists in the subject matter represented by the proposal. It is our responsibility as applicant, then, to take the reader of the proposal step by step through the project activities.

Where

Answering the question *where* will provide the reader of the application a better feel for the proposed project. Will the solution be undertaken in a specific neighborhood? A courthouse? A therapeutic community housed within a medium security correctional facility? The answer to this question implies the physical location of the project. If several locations are involved, we need to make sure each is covered in the description of the solution.

When

As we discuss our plan for solving the problem, it's a good idea to let the funding organization know when the activities will occur. Will this be a 1-year or 2-year project? When will it begin and end? Often, the answer to this question manifests itself in the form of a Gantt chart or similar timetable of project activities. Such a timetable has columns representing major project activities, as well as a column that covers various weeks or months throughout the project. However we decide to present the chronology of the project, it will help the reviewer understand our plan for carrying out in an organized way the many activities that constitute our solution to the problem.

How

Very much related to *what,* the question *how* forces us to make explicit the way in which our proposed project will unfold. For example, if the proposal reviewer knows that data will be gathered as part of the project, we must also walk the reviewer through the process of how this will be accomplished. By surveys? By intensive interviews with clients? In the case of a direct service project, how will the clients get diverted from traditional criminal justice processing to our proposed alternative program? We need to take the reader of the proposal through the process in detail so that he or she will completely understand it from beginning to end. We can't assume that the proposal reader knows how diversion works.

These five questions need not be answered in any particular order. But by the time we have drafted the methods section of our proposal, we should have answered each one.

EXAMPLE 4A: EXPLAINING METHODS FOR A COMMUNITY POLICING PROGRAM

Here, let's return to the law enforcement agency that wants to embrace community policing. Well, to start out, we have a couple of strikes against us. First, if we consult the literature on community policing, we see that it really is more philosophy than programming. This is not easy for a lot of us to grasp, especially those of us who have spent our time implementing concrete, identifiable programs. So looking at our funding proposal from the perspective of the funding organization, we have to ask ourselves what we intend to do that may or may not cost money.

Community policing is often associated with the identification and attention to "broken windows" and other signs of neighborhood decay. Where community policing is sincerely adopted, however, the citizens become the eyes and ears of local law enforcement. In neighborhoods in which drug trafficking is prevalent, for example, citizens become instrumental in assisting law enforcement in identifying crack houses, drug dealers, and other signs of narcotics trafficking. So our methods section must show how we will engage citizens and otherwise involve the "community" in community policing.

One way to address this is to envision how our community policing philosophy will manifest itself. Without new funds, we should be able to assign one or more of our officers to serve in this new role. So what will they be doing in the community that is different from what they did before under more traditional means of policing? Our community policing officers are going to be assigned to specific neighborhoods. We have learned from the community policing literature, as well as from other agencies that have already adopted community policing, that law enforcement officers and the neighborhoods they serve often form a bond when each comes to know the other well. But how can this happen when in our department, officers spend their shifts patrolling in a cruiser?

In our version of community policing, we have decided to put our officers on bicycle, when weather permits. It's much easier for an officer on a bike to stop by and talk to a merchant or other citizen. Officers are more visible this way, and they don't have to concern themselves with parking spaces. Because officer safety is paramount in our hypothetical department, all community policing officers on bikes will wear protective gear, including helmets. The department's insurance company also insists that this happen.

Another facet of our department's commitment to community policing is decentralization. Under the current regime, everyone works out of headquarters, which is located in the downtown area. This is fine for those living and working downtown, but it does nothing to promote better police-community relations with the suburbs and other more outlying areas. Consequently, we want to have small, neighborhood offices where citizens can feel free to stop by and air their concerns. These offices might also have larger rooms where residents can share these concerns and problems at frequent neighborhood meetings.

With our methods section, we should now begin to see a connection between our original problem and our solution. The community policing officers and neighborhood residents with whom they'll have close contact will bond professionally and personally. This, in turn, will heighten the trust that residents have for law enforcement. Consequently, the residents will be more apt to share information about the location of crack houses, the identity of drug dealers and other felons, and other less serious community problems. The officers, in their new community policing role, will respond by using their authority to close crack houses and to arrest those who threaten the safety and sense of well-being in the neighborhood. In addition to their law enforcement role, the officers will also invoke their new problem-solving abilities to address other quality-of-life issues that previously were not the province of the police.

The result of these activities will be a reduction of crime, an improvement in the appearance of the city's neighborhoods, an increase in the perception that the community is safe, and quicker responses to citizen complaints about neighborhood problems. Later, each of these activities can be translated into measurable objectives we formally commit to achieving.

EXAMPLE 4B: EXPLAINING METHODS FOR A PROSECUTOR'S DIVERSION PROGRAM

Now that our hypothetical prosecutor has successfully stated the problem of burgeoning caseloads (Chapter 2), it's time to discuss what we intend to do about it. We already know that we want to implement a diversion program for first-time minor offenders. Once again, the questions this methods section should answer are *who, what, where, when,* and *how.*

For the sake of our example, let's say that our prosecutor's current human and other resources are stretched beyond what is reasonable. Consequently, all staff are busy with other responsibilities. All physical space is occupied. There are barely enough office supplies to serve the current needs of the staff. We should now be getting some ideas about what we need to make our diversion project work.

We will start with the diversion coordinator we want to hire. Because no current staff member can perform these duties, we maintain that we need to bring a new diversion coordinator on board. At this point, we won't go into the qualifications this new hire must have; this will be discussed later in Chapter 7, "Individual and Organizational Capability."

Our next job in helping our hypothetical prosecutor is to discuss exactly what our diversion coordinator will do. Well, we know from the way other diversion programs work that a diversion coordinator's duties often include, but are not necessarily limited to, screening potential clients, counseling them, referring clients to appropriate social services, and maintaining necessary records, as well as checking with local law enforcement agencies and courts to determine if the clients have picked up any new criminal charges during their diversion period. We should go into some detail here. Those who review grant proposals or applications may be generalists. As such, they may not have in-depth knowledge about the way diversion works. To walk them through our diversion process, then, should not be construed as condescending or unnecessary. We want them to understand as much as possible about our proposed solution to make an informed funding decision. Consequently, we will err on the side of giving them more, rather than fewer, details. It makes more work for us, but it will be to our benefit in the long run.

How does our diversion coordinator screen clients for potential participation? What does that mean? It means she will perform additional records checks on all those referred to the program to ensure that they are truly first-time offenders. For those clients who qualify for participation, our diversion coordinator will hold individual and group sessions with them. During the individual sessions, she will learn what types of educational, occupational, and social deficiencies they have that need to be addressed by relevant programming. If such programming goes beyond the knowledge and skills of our diversion coordinator, she will refer the clients to appropriate social service agencies.

Our hypothetical diversion program should also attend to the *when* question. As soon as one of these cases is referred to the prosecutor's office, the record check will be performed. If the record check confirms that the offender is a first-timer, then the assistant prosecutor approaches the offender about participation in the program.

The methods section of this proposal should convince the reader that the glut of minor, nondangerous offenders moving through the prosecutor's office are better addressed through diversion. In theory, the proposed solution will solve the problem by transmitting the values and life skills these offenders need to lead productive, law-abiding lives. We minimize formal intervention in their lives, we reduce their recidivism, and we also save the prosecutor's valuable time for violent and serious cases that do not warrant diversion consideration.

EXAMPLE 4C: EXPLAINING METHODS
FOR A RESTORATIVE JUSTICE PROJECT

Our court that wants to experiment with the concept of restorative justice has, as was stated earlier, a special challenge. Those used to the traditional way of processing criminal cases may be resistant to the whole notion of a different way of doing business. Therefore, we need to take special care to justify everything we believe we need to make such a project work.

For the sake of illustration, let's pretend that the sponsor to whom we intend to send our proposal knows little about restorative justice. Because it is a relatively recent concept, our assumption may be right on the mark. What we need to do, then, is to show exactly how we see our proposed solution working. If we're successful, our methods section will make it obvious that for selected types of cases, our solution is an improvement over conventional processing.

The court will begin by advertising vacancies for an investigator and a restoration counselor. The methods section is not the place to go into detail about the requisite qualifications for these new positions. We will cover that later when we get to "Capabilities." Our project will also build in a modest time within the project period to train new hires both about the local criminal justice system and about their new duties.

Here's how we propose that our hypothetical restorative justice project will work. When a criminal case involving a low-level personal or property crime has had an arraignment, the judge asks both the defendant and the prosecution if they are willing for the case to go to restorative justice. If they are in agreement, the judge permits the restoration counselor to meet with the offender, the prosecutor, the victims, and community representatives to work out a restoration plan through consensus.

Once a case is referred to restorative justice, an investigator begins by interviewing all parties about the circumstances of the alleged offense. From the offender, we get his or her version of the story, as well as relevant social history. The prosecutor relates the official version of the story and asserts what the community should get from any restoration session. The investigator interviews the victim at length to determine the physical, emotional, financial, and other tolls taken by the alleged offense. The investigator also interviews noninvolved citizens regarding their feelings about the offense and their requirements for restoration. Each of these actors finishes the interview by detailing what will bring about true restoration, if it is possible.

On the completion of the interviews, we bring these parties back together. The investigator is present only to clarify results of the investigation. The real work now is to be accomplished by our restoration counselor, whose job it is to achieve consensus among the parties as to what constitutes restoration.

The project we've just described implies several methods that will later translate into specific budget items. At present, the court has neither a restoration counselor nor an investigator. There currently is no available space in the courthouse to permit the interview and restoration sessions. When we hire new personnel, we generally need not only office space but also office furniture, computers and printers, office supplies, funds for necessary travel, and other necessities. The training of the new hires may also require the services of a consulting trainer who helps orient them to their new duties and environment.

Although the definitive answer has to await evaluation results, we at this point should be confident that the problems mentioned in the problem statement have been adequately addressed. Our project was based on the notion that traditional criminal justice processing brings about little satisfaction for the victim, the offender, or the community. If through our case investigations and restoration sessions, we discover what all three parties require to achieve restoration, we should be in a better position to reach some sort of consensus. Victims who get apologies, restitution for losses or harm, or other forms of reparation may well be more satisfied than their counterparts who participate in conventional criminal justice processing. Offenders, too, should benefit from a new system that is designed less to seek retribution and more to habilitate them for productive, law-abiding lifestyles. And the community, seldom seen as a beneficiary of the administration of justice, should be expected to benefit from community service, public apologies, and other more generalized forms of restoration.

EXAMPLE 4D: EXPLAINING METHODS FOR A COMMUNITY-BASED CORRECTIONAL FACILITY PROJECT

Our community-based correctional facility (CBCF) has a plan for how it will reduce the recidivism among residents. The proposed solution to our problem begins with the addition of a classification specialist. This individual will complete a sociolegal dossier on each admission to the program. All these data will be analyzed by the CBCF's statistician using a statistical technique known as cluster analysis. The results of the cluster analyses will determine risk of recidivism. On the basis of this assessment of risk, each resident will be assigned to a specific level of supervision and treatment from the available array of graduated sanctions.

The second important part of our proposed solution to the recidivism problem is the initiation of graduated sanctions. Currently, our program has just two levels of supervision and treatment: minimum and maximum. At the minimum level, offenders are permitted to leave the CBCF for employment purposes. At the maximum level, they cannot leave and also are segregated from the minimum-level residents.

Our program will institute an empirically based typology of CBCF residents. This will be conducted by a consultant who will perform cluster analyses of residents' social, legal, and substance abuse data. Each resulting cluster will represent a group of offenders with distinct attributes, problems, and needs. These, in turn, suggest specific levels in the array of graduated sanctions. Sanctions appropriate for each level will derive from level of drug use, verified criminal history, maturity level, conduct record, and staff recommendations.

The proposed solution in our methods section will show how residents can move up or down through the graduated sanctions, depending on their improvement or setbacks. By having alternatives other than confinement only, we will be able to keep more residents in the CBCF and in treatment, giving us more time to address their respective problems.

5

Objectives and Their Measurement

WHAT ARE OBJECTIVES?

Objectives are statements that reflect the grant applicant's commitment to make some type of measurable progress in implementing the proposed solution to the problem. We know that grant applicants are going to do something; that was made clear in the methods section. But by setting formal objectives, the funding organization can see how much of the proposed intervention will be accomplished within a specified time period.

Strong objectives are measurable. That is, they promise that there will be some level of change as a result of the solution. Typically, the verb in a strong objective suggests that there will be an increase, decrease, reduction, or some other type of change. That is, after all, what our grant proposal is all about. We want our solution to bring about a significant amount of measurable change in the problem.

The more precise we are about the change, the more easily we and others can gauge the extent to which we are successful. Instead of simply saying we will reduce recidivism, we should say by how much we believe we can reduce it. Attaching a number to the objective will also permit an evaluator to measure the extent to which we were successful in addressing the problem.

Those who sponsor projects in criminal justice prefer objectives that lend themselves to measurement. Why? Because this enables them to take stock of how much progress, if any, the applicant eventually makes in solving the problem. Anecdotal and visceral reactions to funded projects may be positive, but today's sponsors respond more strongly to numbers and other empirical evidence. That is why measurable objectives must be part of the proposed project.

It is also critical that the applicant be realistic in committing to a change in measurable indicators of the problem. Objectives that are too modest or too lofty will inadvertently set the applicant up for failure.

Our Protagonist's Objectives

Let's jump back to our suspense novel analogy, in which our protagonist is facing a cataclysmic problem. If the life-or-death problem is not solved, the consequences will be devastating. In grantsmanship, the problem often is less threatening, but the more compelling a problem is, the greater attention it will likely receive from funding organizations.

In our suspense story, as in most suspense tales, there is what novelists refer to as a ticking clock—a time frame in which the problem faced by the protagonist must be solved. If the protagonist fails to meet the deadline—the point at which someone or something literally will be dead—the villain wins. Time, then, is of the essence.

The grant proposal or application also has its ticking clock. The ticking clock is dictated by the length of the grant. This period may be proposed by the applicant or may be set by the funding organization. But we have only a specified time to test our solution to the problem outlined in the problem statement. If we are unsuccessful in solving or at least lessening the problem, we may not get a second year of funding. The objectives section forces us as applicants to implement our solution to the problem within a specific period.

EXAMPLE 5A: OBJECTIVES FOR A COMMUNITY POLICING PROGRAM

Let's go back to our earlier example of community policing. We know what the problem is—crime and social disorganization in a particular neighborhood. And we know what we want to do to solve the problem. We are going to embrace community policing under the premise that if police and community residents become better acquainted, share information, and trust each other more, crime will subside and community development will flourish. But unlike our protagonist who may be able to simply forge ahead in implementing her solution to the life-threatening problem, we as grant applicants have to convince the potential sponsors that our methods are sound. And even after they've approved the plan, they want to see us attain certain milestones along the way.

So what's the first thing we might want to do to prove to the sponsors that we're making good on our solution to crime and social disorder in our community? One part of our strategy is to hold neighborhood meetings to let citizens air their concerns. We even discussed the possibility of having a meeting room in our neighborhood offices for just such a purpose. Our first objective, then, might look like this:

We will hold neighborhood meetings.

One lesson we've learned from funding organizations is that they like to keep track of what we as grantees do. That's why when we get funded, we will have to submit periodic fiscal and programmatic reports. Funding organizations also like for us to measure how much of our solution we've implemented. Now that we know that, we can improve our first draft objective:

We will hold 12 neighborhood meetings.

We are now getting closer to satisfying the sponsor's desire for measurability and specificity. In this example, the sponsor may still wonder when these neighborhood meetings are going to be held. Will we wait until Month 11 of a 1-year project to start holding meetings? If so, we'll have to have roughly 6 meetings in each of the last 2 months. But that never was our intent. Because we are committed to giving the funding organization as much information as it needs, we will be even more specific:

We will hold monthly neighborhood meetings throughout the project period.

This clearly tells the funding organization that there will be at least 12 neighborhood meetings that an evaluator can count. By counting them, we determine the extent to which we've implemented this part of our solution.

As grant applicants pursuing community policing, we would not have to stop here. Many other conceivable objectives could support what we are trying to accomplish. These might include reducing criminal activity by a reasonable amount, cleaning up a specified number of vacant lots, having *x* number of face-to-face meetings with citizens in their homes and businesses, and other related measures.

EXAMPLE 5B: OBJECTIVES FOR A PROSECUTOR'S DIVERSION PROGRAM

For our prosecutor with the unmanageable caseload, we know that we want to implement a diversion program to solve this particular problem. In the methods section, we have detailed how we intend to solve the problem. What remains now is to break down the solution into specific, measurable activities. One of these might be this:

We will divert at least five qualifying cases per month from traditional prosecution.

This is a start. No diversion program will work without clients, so this is a reasonable objective. Keeping in mind the overall solution we proposed for our problem, however, we might offer yet another objective:

We will hold weekly classes on job interviewing, financial management, conflict resolution, and parenting for diverted offenders.

The advantage of the last objective is that it begins to go beyond pure implementation measures and moves toward client outcomes based on program services. Why should it be important to put client services in our objective? Because we earlier argued that such services will help to turn these minor offenders into productive, law-abiding citizens. Although the process of getting referrals is important to measure, our sponsor will ultimately be much more interested in what we actually do for the offenders we divert. We as prosecutors promoting the diversion know that simply routing offenders away from conventional processing often is not enough by itself. Not only do other diversion programs give first-time offenders a second chance, but also they typically make use of relevant programming to decrease the probability of recidivism. Let's say for the sake of our example that our offender pool is made up of young men and women who lack gainful employment and other life skills. We stated earlier that we would address those deficiencies through structured sessions on job interviewing, financial management, conflict resolution, and parenting skills. The diversion coordinator we intend to hire will be adept at delivering such services or referring clients to other agencies that can meet these needs.

There is no magic number of objectives we should put into our proposal. But because we argued in the problem statement that the prosecutor has been mired in the processing of minor, nonviolent offenders, we probably should commit to an objective that will demonstrate the extent to which our solution will address workload issues:

Our proposed project will result in a 10% decrease in the number of formally prosecuted cases for third- and fourth-degree felony offenders as measured by monthly caseload statistics.

The above set of objectives thus addresses both process and outcome measures. There is sufficient detail in them that an evaluator could now devise an evaluation plan to determine the extent to which our solution does or does not solve the problem we discussed in the problem statement.

Here, too, are opportunities for additional objectives. The diversion program could commit to objectives relating to restitution for victims, hours spent in community service, reducing recidivism, numbers of referrals to other social services, and other reasonable outcomes for a diversion program.

EXAMPLE 5C: OBJECTIVES FOR A RESTORATIVE JUSTICE PROJECT

In our restorative justice project, we are starting a new program where one did not exist before. As such, we are likely to encounter a number of problems. One such problem is that there may be few programs from which we can borrow proved measurable objectives. This will require some creativity on our part.

Because we value the importance of evaluation, we will commit to a process evaluation, which will be discussed later in this chapter. A process evaluation should begin as soon as possible. Some evaluators even argue that such an evaluation should begin before the actual project begins, inasmuch as certain issues that predate the project startup can have an impact on its implementation. Because we've already committed to a process evaluation, we ask ourselves questions that relate strictly to project implementation.

Have we hired qualified staff?

If we've failed to bring on board someone who's qualified to investigate the cases being referred for restorative justice, we could conceivably be striking restoration agreements based on erroneous information.

Have we started the project on time?

A number of factors can affect the actual start-up of a criminal justice project. One might be the flow of funds to pay for personnel, rent, and equipment. Another could be the disorganization or ineptitude of those administering the project. In any case, has our project started when we promised it would? If not, what were the reasons for the delay? Our process evaluation will tell where we went wrong in getting started on time.

Have we appropriately identified participants?

Our restorative justice project rests on the assumption that the restoration of victim, offender, and the community better serves the ends of justice than a more traditional, retributive stance. But not everyone subscribes to such a new brand of justice. It's therefore incumbent on us as project directors to make sure we've identified parties who are amenable to restorative justice.

If, when we hold a restorative justice session, victims lash out not only at the offender but also at the project staff because they feel that they can never be restored to the state they enjoyed prior to the crime, then we probably have made a serious process error. Here we may not have done a sufficient job of screening victims for participation.

But what of outcome or impact measures for our project? Surely, we should be confident enough in this new brand of justice to commit to one or more outcome measures. Funding agencies will expect it. One such objective might read something like this:

> The proposed project will bring about in restorative justice participants a 25% increase in the satisfaction with the outcome of the criminal case.

To test this objective, we might want our evaluator to compare the satisfaction level of our program participants with a matched sample of those who experience traditional criminal case processing. Another tack might be to look at satisfaction levels of participants before and after a restoration session. In devising objectives, it helps to think about how we might want to evaluate our program. This, in turn, helps generate good ideas for measurable objectives.

EXAMPLE 5D: OBJECTIVES
FOR A COMMUNITY-BASED
CORRECTIONAL FACILITY PROJECT

Recidivism is at the heart of our CBCF project. Offenders who commit a new offense or a technical violation such as a dirty drug screen are failures from our point of view. We don't want failures. Many of the other correctional alternatives have significantly high rates of recidivism. Much of the reason we exist, then, is to set our particular form of correctional programming apart from the other less-than-successful programs.

Because recidivism is the main problem driving our quest for funds, we can start by translating it into a measurable objective:

> We will reduce the recidivism of our residents by 20% during the project period.

Here we would compare the data from our project with baseline data from the year before. The difference between the two would reveal the extent to which our project actually reduced recidivism among our CBCF residents.

We could arbitrarily come up with more objectives for our CBCF project. The above objective, however, is without question the most important milestone we want to achieve with our solution. The development of further objectives could continue with those relating to reducing the "dirty urines" of drug-addicted clients, increasing their gainful employment, and other means of establishing that our CBCF is improving its success.

EVALUATING THE OBJECTIVES

Evaluations give projects a certain credibility. If a project team is willing to subject its project to empirical scrutiny, prospective sponsors may interpret this as a sincere commitment to making an important contribution to the field. It sends the dual message that the team wants to know what it is doing wrong so it can be corrected and what it is doing right so it can be shared with other criminal justice professionals.

There are two types of evaluation with which grant seekers should be concerned. Both were mentioned earlier—*process evaluation* and *outcome evaluation*.

What Is a Process Evaluation?

A process evaluation is a systematic examination of how a project is implemented. Everything connected to the proposed project, from the initial hiring of staff to the way clients are referred to a program, is fair game for a process evaluation. In a process evaluation, the objective is to determine if the entire process of the project is being carried out as proposed.

Process evaluations are important for the success of a funded project. For one, by dissecting the processes of a project, the evaluator can say what went wrong in the implementation of the project. For another, process evaluations are also important in that they tell the project manager what adjustments need to be made to get the project to work the way it originally was proposed.

In the diversion example, a process evaluation would ask if staff has been hired. Has the office space been rented? If our diversion program depends on clients from local law enforcement agencies, then the process evaluation will reveal whether clients are actually being referred by law enforcement. If equipment is part of the proposed project, the process evaluation will show whether it has been ordered, installed, and used by project staff. These process questions need to be asked and answered. Why? Because if the process of hiring, equipment ordering, and client referral break down, the rest of our proposed solution will not be possible.

What Is an Outcome or Impact Evaluation?

The other main type of evaluation is called an outcome or impact evaluation. Impact evaluations tell both project staff and project sponsors what type of impact, if any, the project in question has had on the problem that spawned the project in the first place.

Outcome evaluations generally are considered more important in that they tell us what works in criminal justice. Knowing what works keeps criminal justice practitioners from wasting resources on programming that is inert. Some types of programming could even be harmful to the population they were designed to help. We also need to know what works in the field so that we can confidently replicate elsewhere solutions that show positive results, or at least the promise of them.

For example, if a community-based correctional treatment program commits to reducing recidivism by 10%, a check of rearrests for the treatment group might reveal that the outcome was a reduction of only 7%. This part of the evaluation usually is most closely tied to the measurable objectives discussed above.

Who Should Conduct the Evaluation?

It is preferable if a neutral third party conducts the evaluation. This gives the project more credibility. If this is not possible, then the project staff should still undertake an evaluation, perhaps in collaboration with the sponsoring foundation or agency, if the latter has the resources to assist. The proposed work will give alternative means of staffing evaluation efforts, including the use of student interns and volunteers.

As mentioned above, in-house evaluations may be perceived as somewhat self-serving at best, and at worst, dishonest. Not all grant applicants conducting their own evaluations are automatically suspect; if perception is everything, or at least a lot of it, however, then the applicant may want to shy away from this approach. This problem is somewhat analogous to the position of auditor. Auditors from outside the organization they are auditing probably are deemed more independent and objective than auditors from inside the organization.

If resources are available, the grant applicant should try to contract with a reputable, outside firm to perform the evaluation. This is seldom inexpensive. Academic institutions and private research firms often have evaluation experts who are experienced in carrying out complex program assessments. Still, when one considers the benefits derived from a thorough, objective assessment of a criminal justice project, the costs to the applicant and to the field in general may be modest.

6

The Budget and Budget Narrative

The budget may be the least favorite part of a grant proposal to prepare, but it is among the most important. In the budget, the prospective sponsor discovers how much the solution as detailed in the methods section will cost. Typically, these include, but are not necessarily limited to, personnel, equipment, supplies, contractual items, consultants, and travel. Each needs a cost attached that is reasonable. In addition to detailing what the sponsor is expected to contribute, a budget should show the contributions of other project sponsors.

As important as the budget itself is the budget narrative. This tells in words what the budget tells in numbers. But it is not simply a duplication of information. The budget narrative also explains and, in some cases, justifies each item in the budget. Simply listing the items may not make it clear how each fits into the overall project. A good budget narrative goes a step further and shows how the applicant arrived at the numbers. A carefully written budget narrative can also help the potential sponsor understand why all the personnel, equipment, consultants, supplies, and travel expenses are necessary to solve the problem originally detailed in the problem statement. Again, keep in mind that the story about our problem should be as evident in our budget as it is in the problem statement.

As grant applicants, we should request funds for only what we really need. There is always the temptation to request funds for those things we want but that may not necessarily be related to our original problem. For example, both academicians and practitioners belong to professional organizations. These associations and societies usually hold annual meetings, sometimes in cities far more exotic than those in which we live. So there is a human temptation to include such trips in a grant proposal or application because we need the money for them.

The same can be said for personal computers. Even in an era in which personal computers are commonplace, some requests for them may not be well justified. For example, take the case of the small-town police department or big-city grassroots community organization. Both may be operating on the proverbial shoestring budget and therefore not have money to buy computers. Through a grant application, they naturally see an opportunity to get this much-needed computer hardware and software. The problem here is that in the case of the professional trip and the personal computer, neither one is automatically necessary to undertake the proposed solution. If the item is necessary to help solve the problem, it should be in the budget—adequately explained and justified. If the solution will work without the item, the grant seeker is well advised to omit it.

WHAT ARE THE BUDGET CATEGORIES?

There are several standard budget categories that applicants tend to see in most grant applications or solicitations. These vary, however, from funding organization to funding organization. The categories discussed in this book should be considered generic and are used solely for illustration. Those completing real applications or proposals should use the specific categories set out by the funding organization. If the organization does not have a standard set of budget categories, the ones listed here should serve the applicant's purposes.

Personnel

This section of the budget represents the staff members who will be working on the proposed project. Personnel includes those persons who will be staffing the project full-time or part-time. It does not, however, include consultants to the project or those who may be affiliated with the project as contractors. These contributors will be covered in other sections of the budget.

In general, the personnel section consists of salary and benefits. The salary is the amount of money paid to regular project staff in return for the work they perform. It is also usual and customary to request the funding agency to cover the staff person's regular benefits for the amount of time the person is contributing to the proposed project. These benefits may include health insurance, retirement contributions, workers' compensation contributions, and other normal benefits that ordinarily accrue to the staff member. Some funding organizations require that the benefits be subdivided into all their constituent parts (health insurance, workers' compensation, etc.), each with its own percentage and cost. Applicants should always check the requirements of the funding organization before preparing the budget.

Example: Personnel
Project Director, $2,400 per month for 12 months	$28,800
Benefits @ 34% of $28,800	$9,792
Personnel subtotal	$38,592

Equipment

Often, a proposed demonstration or research project requires some type of equipment. For example, researchers evaluating a court delay project might want to supply the court with a computer and software dedicated to entering the evaluation data. If the solution developed by a multijurisdictional law enforcement task force for combating drug trafficking requires infrared night vision goggles, then the goggles would be listed in the equipment section of the budget.

The budget for equipment simply consists of the purchase price for which the sponsor's grant is responsible. If the crime lab in a sheriff's office needs a mass spectrometer to perform chemical analyses of crime evidence, applicants should list the cost of such equipment. The equipment budget is not the place to put maintenance contracts, although they may be necessary for keeping equipment in operating condition. Any contracts belong in the contractual section, which is discussed later.

Example: Equipment
DataQuest portable computer	$3,299
LaserBeam printer	$799
Equipment subtotal	$4,098

Supplies

Most criminal justice projects require at least some supplies. Whether these are common office supplies such as photocopy and fax paper, printer cartridges, floppy diskettes, pens, markers, or flip charts, most projects demand a certain modicum of supplies, unless these are being contributed to the project by the applicant.

Most sponsors do not expect the applicant to list in minute detail the cost of every tablet and box of staples. This would demand too much work by the applicant, and it would provide much more detail than that required or even desired by the sponsor. Suffice it to say that grant-making organizations expect to pay for reasonable supplies necessary for carrying out the proposed project.

Example: Supplies
Miscellaneous office supplies	$200
Postage, 2,000 pieces @ $.33 per piece	$660
Supplies subtotal	$860

Travel

Travel consists of the costs associated with any travel implied by the methods section. If researchers are going to evaluate seven pilot projects, each of which is located in a community other than the one in which they live, the sponsor knows that travel will be involved.

Normally, travel has several components including airfare, auto-related expenses, meals or travel per diems, and ground transportation. Although there is no proper order, airfare often is listed first, presumably because it generally will be the most expensive component of the travel budget. Airfare is normally determined by a call to a travel agent or airline. The applicant will discover that the cost depends on variables such as advance reservations, Saturday night stayovers, and special deals offered by the airlines. It is recommended that the cost for such arrangements be kept as minimal as possible; any travel involving flights will likely receive close scrutiny by those reading the grant application.

Example: Travel

Round-trip airfare to Lansing, MI	$282
1,500 miles in personal auto @ $.28 per mile	$420
Per diem, 4 days @ $95 per day	$380
Travel subtotal	$1,082

Contractual Items

A number of project necessities can come under this heading. Office space is often a subject of contract between the applicant organization and the company from which it leases its space. This, then, is a justifiable expense if the applicant organization is unable to contribute this to the project.

Equipment maintenance is another expense that criminal justice projects may encounter. If personal computers, printers, photocopiers, portable telephones, and other such equipment are part of a proposed project, then the maintenance of them could be important to the success of the project. This often is covered by maintenance contracts that may be included in the project's budget.

Example: Contractual Items

Office space, 5,000 sq. ft. @ $1 per sq. ft. per month for 12 months	$60,000
AmeriPhone cellular service @ $27.50 per month for 12 months	$330
Printing	$275
Contractual items subtotal	$60,605

Consultants

At times, a project team may need the services of a consultant. An example of this is the criminological research project that requires a statistician to help draw a representative sample of cases for study. Practitioners often tread into unfamiliar territory with newly funded projects. It is not uncommon, then, for them to enlist a known expert who can help them effectively and efficiently implement the solution in question. Examples of areas in which consultants are commonly used in criminal justice include community policing, community corrections, program evaluation, drug courts, restorative justice, minority overrepresentation, and, of course, grantsmanship.

Example: Consultants

Statistical consulting, 40 hours @ $35 per hour	$1,400
Consulting psychologist, 200 hours @ $85 per hour	$17,000
Consultant subtotal	$18,400

IN-KIND AND MATCH CONTRIBUTIONS

Some applicants attempting to get grant funds may have some, but not all, of the resources necessary to carry out the proposed project. From the sponsor's point of view, applicants who are contributing some of their own resources look better than those expecting the sponsor to foot the entire bill. Contributions that an applicant is making other than cash are termed *in-kind* contributions. These can include personnel, equipment, supplies, and any of the other budget categories items.

In-kind contributions consist of human and other resources that applicants are able to devote to the proposed project. Again, applicants' attempt to contribute some of their own resources to the proposed solution is often perceived as a plus in the eyes of potential funding organizations.

In-kind contributions can and should be reflected in the grant proposal if the format permits. Often, this can be accomplished simply by adding another column in the budget titled "In-Kind." This signals to the reader of the proposal or application that those resources in the in-kind column are being contributed by the applicant. As such, those figures, although part of the total project cost, are not part of the formal grant request.

Match, which is also a contribution the applicant makes to a proposed project, differs in that it is required by the funding organization. The Byrne Memorial State and Local Law Enforcement Assistance Program, for example, requires a 25% cash match from those who receive funding through this program. This is not optional. Applicants for funding, therefore, should always check to see if matching funds are required.

In some cases, the required match may be in-kind. This generally is easier for an applicant to contribute than cash match.

WHAT IS A BUDGET NARRATIVE?

A budget narrative builds on the numerical information in the budget. Although the numbers tell the prospective sponsor how much the applicant wants for each item in the budget, the budget narrative explains how the numbers were derived. As such, the narrative forms a connective tissue between the original problem and the budget request. This connective tissue is important because it shows in plain language why each budget item is critical to solving the problem.

In the format of a grant proposal or application, the budget narrative typically follows the budget. By building on the examples used throughout the book, the following will show how the budget and budget narrative blend together to tell the prospective sponsor not only how much money is needed to implement the proposed solution but also how these figures were established and why the items are necessary.

EXAMPLE 6A: BUDGET AND BUDGET NARRATIVE FOR A COMMUNITY POLICING PROGRAM

Budget

Personnel
Not applicable. [Here we've chosen not to include the cost of personnel primarily because the literature on community policing suggests that we can undertake this new philosophy without additional hires.]

Equipment

Trailmaster trail bicycles, 12 @ $495 per unit	$5,940
Protective gear and helmets, 12 @ $119 per set	$1,428
Equipment subtotal	$7,368

Supplies

Card stock for citizen comment cards	$74

Travel

Hotel, 3 nights @ $85 per night	$255

Contractual Items

Neighborhood office rent, $.75 per sq. ft. per month	
150 sq. ft. 12 months 3 offices	$4,050
Bicycle maintenance contracts, 12 @ $50 per unit	$600
Cellular phones, 12 @ $65 per month per unit 12 months	$9,360
Contractual items subtotal	$14,010

Consultants

Dr. Norman Farley, 15 days @ $225 per day	$3,375
Budget total	$25,082

Budget Narrative

Personnel
> Not applicable

Equipment
> The price for these bicycles was established by the lowest bid of those solicited by the Department of Public Safety from local bicycle shops. The bicycles will be used by the 12 community policing officers participating in the proposed project.

Travel
> The travel is necessary to attend the State Community Policing Convention held in the state capital. This hotel rate is the special rate given to convention attendees.

Supplies
> The card stock will be used to print our citizen comment cards to be handed out by the community policing officers. The price comes from the catalog of the city's office supply company under term contract.

Contractual Items
> To serve neighborhood residents where they live, the project will rent office space in each of the neighborhoods to be served. The cost represents an average of the square footage cost of the offices in question, each of which is significantly below normal office space cost in the city.

Consultants
> Dr. Farley, nationally recognized expert on community policing, will assist the department with the revision of its mission statement, policies and procedures, and rules of officer conduct to be consistent with the philosophy of community policing. The rate of $225 is the normal rate that Dr. Farley charges for his services and is consistent with fees usually charged by others with his level of expertise.

EXAMPLE 6B: BUDGET AND BUDGET NARRATIVE FOR A PROSECUTOR'S DIVERSION PROGRAM

Budget

Personnel

Diversion Coordinator, 2,080 hours @ $16.25 per hour	$33,800
Secretary, 520 hours @ $11.72 per hour	$6,094
Personnel subtotal	$39,894

Equipment

Personal computer, 1 @ $2,799	$2,799
Laser printer, 1 @ $499	$499
Equipment subtotal	$3,298

Travel
  Personal auto, 400 miles @ $.32 per mile $128
Supplies
  Misc. office supplies (paper, laser cartridges, etc.) $80
Contractual Items
  Not applicable
Consultants
  Not applicable
              Budget total $43,400

Budget Narrative

Personnel

The diversion coordinator will be paid at the standard starting rate for nonlegal, professional employees of the prosecutor's office. The secretary for this project will serve the proposed project at 25% of full-time. These salary figures include regular employee benefits including health and dental insurance, workers' compensation, retirement system contribution, and prepaid legal services.

Equipment

The prices of the computer and printer were determined by the price of those recently purchased for the prosecutor's office. These will be used to maintain program records and generate periodic reports to the prosecutor and to the sponsor.

Travel

The diversion coordinator will incur area mileage from making arrangements with social services agencies, taking clients to appointments, and other routine auto travel. The rate of $.32 per mile is that established for county employees.

Supplies

These include normal office supplies such as computer paper, sticky notes, pens, and legal pads. These will be purchased through the county's contracted office supplier.

Contractual Items

Not applicable

Consultants

Not applicable

EXAMPLE 6C: BUDGET AND BUDGET NARRATIVE FOR A RESTORATIVE JUSTICE PROJECT

Budget

Personnel
  Restoration Counselor, 2,080 hours @ $18.75 per hour $39,000
    Benefits @ 30% of salary $11,700

Investigator, 2,080 hours @ $15.80 per hour	$32,864
Benefits @ 30% of salary	$9,859
Personnel subtotal	$93,423

Equipment

Personal computer, 1 @ $1,995	$1,995
Tape recorder with transcription equipment, 1 @ $139	$139
Equipment subtotal	$2,134

Travel

Airfare (round-trip) to Washington, D.C.	$135

Supplies

Office supplies (audiotapes, computer paper, etc.)	$80

Contractual Items

Office space, 160 sq. ft. @ $.90 per sq. ft. per month 12 months	$1,728
Computer service contract, $12 per month 12 months	$144
Contractual items subtotal	$1,872

Consultants

Not applicable	
Budget total	$97,644

Budget Narrative

Personnel

Compensation for the restoration counselor was determined by the Civil Service Commission. The salary for the investigator represents the rate for other entry-level investigators in county government.

Equipment

The personal computer is necessary for the transcribing of notes from the restoration conferences. The price reflects the lowest available from local vendors. The transcribing equipment, necessary for the preservation of restoration agreements, will be purchased from the county's office supply contractor.

Travel

The restoration counselor will travel to Washington, D.C., to the Restoration Workshop sponsored by the National Center for Juvenile Alternatives. This workshop will cover both the philosophy and application of restorative justice. The restoration counselor will earn continuing education units for attending.

Supplies

This budget item will cover such routine office supplies as pens, legal tablets, paper clips, and file folders. It will also cover the cost of audiotapes used to record the restoration sessions.

Contractual Items

The cost for the office space is normal for space in or near the central business district. The contract for the computer maintenance, also under county term contract, is necessary because the county does not have a qualified computer repair person on staff.

Consultants
   Not applicable

EXAMPLE 6D: BUDGET AND BUDGET NARRATIVE FOR A COMMUNITY-BASED CORRECTIONAL FACILITY PROJECT

Budget

Personnel
   Classification Specialist, 2,080 hours @ $22.50 per hour $46,800
      Benefits @ 34% of salary $15,912
         Personnel subtotal $62,712
Equipment
   Personal computer, 1 @ $2,145 $2,145
Travel
   Not applicable
Supplies
   Statistical software $700
Contractual Items
   Not applicable
Consultants
   Roger McCluster, M.A., 40 hours @ $30 per hour $1,200
      Budget total $66,757

Budget Narrative

Personnel
   The salary is in line with the facility's pay scale for an entry-level classification specialist. There are no scheduled pay raises during the project period.
Equipment
   The personal computer will allow program staff to keep detailed records for the cluster analyses. It will also be used to perform the actual cluster analyses.
Travel
   Not applicable
Supplies
   Statistical Software for Corrections will be used to perform the cluster analyses necessary for classification.
Contractual Items
   Not applicable
Consultants
   The services of Roger McCluster, M.A., will be engaged to train the classification specialist in the application of statistical clustering to offender classification. Mr. McCluster's rate is customary for such services and is supported by his curriculum vitae.

7

Individual and Organizational Capability

Individual Capability

Prospective sponsors want to know that there will be staff qualified and competent enough to successfully implement the solution to the problem. It is one thing to write a grant proposal; it is clearly another to make good on the promise. Funding organizations, then, are concerned that the project team is capable of carrying out the proposed project. This is true not only for research projects that tend to be more technical in nature but also for demonstration and direct service projects that serve specific target populations. The sponsor needs to know that those who will staff a proposed project can carry out the plan as laid out in the proposal.

This part of the proposal is a place for factual descriptions of the project staff—not a place for exaggerations. Many funding organizations make use of outside reviewers to evaluate grant applications and proposals. These reviewers often will know if applicants are being honest about their qualifications. The information included in this section, therefore, should be limited to the accurate, relevant background of all project staff.

Just as applicants should be honest, they should also provide what is necessary and no more. In keeping with the analogy of the suspense novel, let's imagine a courtroom scene. In this courtroom is a law enforcement officer on the witness stand about to be grilled by a sharp, high-priced defense attorney. When asked about her qualifications to investigate the alleged crime, does the officer ramble on about her volunteer work at the local zoo? You bet not. It's not relevant to the point at hand. The officer relates only that information that speaks to her expertise as a detective.

Now back to our grant application: In stating qualifications for conducting the proposed project, we should stick to just what is relevant. What qualifications of the staff person are requisite for performing the project activities and meeting the objectives? Again, it matters little to the funding organization that the staff person won third prize in a woodworking contest. That may be nice, but it's not pertinent to the problem and solution at hand.

If the format of the grant proposal or application permits, we should include résumés or curricula vitae as appendixes. This keeps what might be rather lengthy documents from interrupting the flow of the proposal or application.

Some application or proposal formats call for a section on staff qualifications. If this is the case, then we should summarize the relevant material from the résumés in paragraph form. To an extent, space will dictate what we can include in such a summary. The best advice is to stick with the staff qualifications that are most relevant to the proposed methods.

What Should Be Included in a Résumé?

A résumé is a brief summary of a person's qualifications. Formats vary for résumés, but in general they contain the following information.

Heading

This section at the top of the résumé includes the staff person's name, address, telephone numbers, and e-mail address, if applicable.

Objective

Although a statement of objectives is often found on résumés of staff, especially those seeking employment, it is not important for the purposes of establishing qualifications for our grant proposal.

Background Summary

This section summarizes the staff person's experience. It should briefly show why the individual is qualified for the role he or she hopes to play in the funded project. Sometimes, this summary is written in narrative form; it may also be structured as a short, bulleted list.

Accomplishments

Some résumés have this section to point out the staff person's major professional achievements. This may take the form of previous problems the staff member has solved, perhaps with indicators of how these milestones were measured.

Professional Experience

This need be nothing more than a reverse chronological listing of the positions the staff member has held in recent years. It should also mention the organizations worked for, the years employed, and the locations.

Education

This section should contain a brief but complete listing of the staff person's education background. Each entry should include the degree earned, the major, the institution, and the year.

Personal Interests

As with résumés designed for job seekers, this information is optional. It probably will be less important to grant reviewers than the other information listed above.

ORGANIZATIONAL CAPABILITY

Just as the qualifications of individual staff members are important to funding entities, so is the capability of the organization seeking the funds. Sponsors are looking for good investments of their funds, and part of the decision rests on the strength and character of the applicant organization. The more the applicant organization can attest to its reputation, the better the funding agency is likely to feel about putting its money in the applicant's stewardship.

Organizational capability probably means different things to different people. Still, it comprises several common attributes. These include the age, size, funding base, and accomplishments of the organization. Why should the age of an organization be important? Well, on one count, the older an organization is, the more stable it is perceived to be. And the more stable it is thought to be, so the argument goes, the better suited it is as a recipient of a grant to perform a demonstration or research project.

EXAMPLE 7A: DOCUMENTING CAPABILITY
FOR A COMMUNITY POLICING PROGRAM

Organizational Capability

The job for us on this project is to show that the law enforcement agency applying for the grant is worthy and capable of such an award. This section should describe the department in great detail. Some of these details might include the level of government in which it is located, the size of the staff, the annual budget, and the extent to which it's accredited.

Once we've acquainted the grant reviewer with the basics of our department and the community in which it's located, it might not be a bad idea to brag a little about any distinguishing features. Has our law enforcement agency achieved accreditation? A lot of police departments and sheriff's offices consider this important. Have any of the agency's employees been cited for bravery, exemplary citizenship, or other noteworthy awards?

Has our department received any other grants? If so, what distinguishing accomplishments resulted from these monies? Were the grant fiscal and programmatic reports all submitted on time? This may sound trivial, but to the funding organization, it may suggest that the department has responsibly administered grant funds for important purposes in the past, making it a good risk for the current request.

Staff Qualifications

We know that 12 of our officers will be assigned to this project. If we know which ones, is there anything we can say about them that sets them apart from their counterparts? Are they more experienced? Have any or all received specialized training, perhaps at the FBI Academy or other prestigious center? Have they received any awards from the department or community for distinguished service?

EXAMPLE 7B: DOCUMENTING CAPABILITY
FOR A PROSECUTOR'S DIVERSION PROGRAM

Organizational Capability

By virtue of the respect their office commands, prosecutors do not have a tough case to make when it comes to capability. Still, there are a number of ways we can describe the office to bolster its case for funding.

Prosecutors generally have a specified time to try criminal cases. Has our prosecutor successfully prosecuted all criminal cases without losing any to statutory time limits? And what of prior grants? Is there a history, even a short one, that shows the office's ability to secure and manage grant funds? Has our prosecutor instituted any new programs since elected? Is so, what are these programs, and what has been their effect on the administration of criminal justice?

Staff Qualifications

In our hypothetical example, we need someone who can run our diversion program. More important, however, we need to show that the individual who will staff the project will be able to undertake all the project activities discussed in the methods section.

Regarding academic credentials, we probably would want a staff member with a degree in the social or behavioral sciences. This includes sociology, criminology, criminal justice, social work, and other related areas.

We might also want someone for the job other than a recent graduate. This is not to imply that we should eliminate inexperienced, new graduates from consideration. It's only to say that our proposed project might be better served by someone who knows his or her way around local criminal justice systems. As such, the individual would be acquainted with the concept of diversion, grand juries and the indictment process, available social service agencies, and a host of other relevant factors.

EXAMPLE 7C: DOCUMENTING CAPABILITY FOR A RESTORATIVE JUSTICE PROJECT

Organizational Capability

Almost by definition, courts demonstrate organizational capability. The prestige that typically accompanies judges and their courts nearly eliminates the need to build a case for it. Still, there are opportunities for acquainting the proposal reader with this particular court and what may set it apart from others.

Our discussion, of course, can include the size and diversity of the staff. How many judges are there? Is there a court administrator? What is the criminal and civil caseload of late? We could also include the court's annual budget.

Staff Qualifications

Our restorative justice project calls for two positions. One is the investigator, the other the restoration counselor. Each of these positions will require its own case for expertise.

In the case of the investigator, we want to show that the person to be hired is qualified for the position. If we don't know who eventually will hold the position, then we need to show the requisite qualifications. These would undoubtedly include investigative experience as gained from a position in law enforcement, for example.

The qualifications for our restoration counselor might include experience in dispute resolution and conflict management. It may also include service as a victim advocate to ensure that the restoration process is sensitive to the unique needs of crime victims. Regarding education, we might expect our restoration counselor to hold at least a bachelor's degree in social work or counseling, and perhaps even a master's in one of these fields.

EXAMPLE 7D: DOCUMENTING CAPABILITY FOR A COMMUNITY-BASED CORRECTIONAL FACILITY PROJECT

Organizational Capability

We'll pretend the CBCF in question has been in existence for 7 years. Its administrator reports to a board of directors that oversees the operation of the facility. In its 7 years of operation, the CBCF has managed to increase its operating budget each year by an average of 16%.

The State Board of Correctional Inspectors rates the CBCF as a Four Star Facility, meaning that it has met their highest standards of public safety, accountability, and cleanliness.

Staff Qualifications

Our director will manage the proposed project to address recidivism among the CBCF's residents. He has 18 years of correctional experience, the last 7 as administrator of the CBCF. He holds a B.A. in criminal justice from Michigan State University, an M.S.W. from The Ohio State University, and an M.P.A. from Central Michigan University. A licensed alcohol and substance abuse counselor, he frequently consults on community-based corrections for other jurisdictions.

8

Preparing the Research Proposal

A research proposal in criminal justice or criminology is different from a program proposal. As such, it has a different structure and different requirements. It is similar, however, in that it also is intended to solve a problem. But research problems are more information problems than they are people problems.

MAKING THE CASE FOR A RESEARCH OR AN EVALUATION PROJECT

In general, the problem in a research or an evaluation project is grounded in a gap in knowledge. The gap can be a void in the empirical literature that the applicant intends to fill. Or it can be a gap in knowledge about whether a criminal justice intervention program works. In both cases, the problem to be solved is a lack of knowledge that the applicant wants to remedy.

In making the case for a research study, we must discuss the relevant theoretical and research literature to date. Through such a discussion, we show a series of building blocks, each of which raises the wall of knowledge by another row. The next empirical step that we want to take to advance knowledge in the field will add another row to this empirical wall.

For the evaluation project in criminal justice, our rationale differs somewhat from that of the research project. Instead of appealing solely to gaps in the literature, part of the answer is to be found in why we conduct any evaluations. Quite simply, we want to know what works. Once we do, we can more confidently replicate promising criminal justice programs in other jurisdictions.

The other part of the answer lies in the consequences of not having good evaluative information. As discussed in Chapter 5, "Objectives and Their Meas-

urement," evaluation results permit us to identify problems in the implementation of a direct service project. Such problems can compromise an entire program if they go undiagnosed and unattended. So it benefits us greatly to learn
early what's wrong with our process so we can correct it and meet our objectives.

EXPLAINING METHODS FOR A
RESEARCH OR AN EVALUATION PROJECT

The methods section of a research project is extremely important. Even if the
problem statement portion of the application or proposal has been brilliantly argued, the methods section can kill the chances for funding if not done well. Part
of doing it well is being specific and detailed about how the research will be
conducted.

For a research project, we don't have to go into much detail about the notion
that one or more researchers will be doing the work. Most sponsors and their
proposal review committees make that inferential leap. This sounds as if it con-
tradicts what's been discussed in the other examples. It does somewhat, but research and evaluation projects, in general, must be looked at a bit differently
from the way we view their direct service counterparts. That someone will be
performing the research should be understood. Details about their qualifications
will be discussed in the section on capabilities.

Research and evaluation projects depend on data. This information can be
so-called secondary data, or it can be data that are being gathered for the first
time. The point is that the funding organization is going to where it's coming
from. Are the necessary data housed at the Inter-University Consortium for Political and Social Research at the University of Michigan? If so, will the applicant simply analyze data that have already been collected? Or alternatively, if
the data have not yet been collected, how will this be accomplished?

Again, more, rather than fewer, details will serve the applicant's needs. If the
data are to be collected through a random telephone survey, how will the researcher ensure that the resultant sample is representative of the population being studied? Researchers in general, and specifically those serving as grant proposal reviewers, expect these issues to be laid out in considerable detail. Is this
because researchers are trained to attend to details that would bore the layper-
son? Perhaps. But a more plausible explanation for this insistence on detail is
that the methods by which research data are gathered impinge on their validity
and reliability. Data gathered in a careless or otherwise nonscientific way may
well be useless in addressing the issues discussed in the problem statement. And
after all, that's the purpose of going to all this trouble of laying out a possible
solution.

After the discussion of how the data will be gathered, it's a good idea to spend
some time on the structure of the data. Again, the researchers on the proposal re-

view team may put themselves in the position of the applicant, which prompts them to pose the same questions that the applicant should be asking.

By asking the following questions, we as applicants can be sure that we have adequately discussed the data to be collected and analyzed:

- What is the name of the variable?
- How is the variable defined?
- What are the values of each variable?
- What level of measurement (nominal, ordinal, etc.) is the variable?

There is a strong link between the type of data and the way data should be analyzed. For example, if we propose to perform linear regression on the data in question, the data have to be of a level of measurement that permits such analyses. It then is up to us to make sure that the proposal reviewers can see that the data to be gathered can be analyzed with the statistical methods to be applied. Once again, as applicants, we should expect the proposal reviewers to know as much as or perhaps even more about our subject matter than we do. Even if this isn't true, if we approach the methods section in this way, the result will be much stronger.

Specificity is the rule for describing proposed statistical analyses. Too many grant applicants for research projects hurt their chances by using vague verbiage to describe statistical procedures. A common phrase found in research proposals is "appropriate multivariate techniques." This may be perceived by grant reviewers as "the researchers really haven't a clue which techniques they're going to use." If the research project is well planned, we should be able to say with precision exactly which statistical methods we intend to employ. Instead of a vague reference to nonspecific methods, we should spend time discussing the way we intend to use factor analysis, for example, to understand the underlying structure of the data.

DOCUMENTING CAPABILITY FOR A RESEARCH OR AN EVALUATION PROJECT

Organizational Capability

For purposes of illustration, let's say that our applicant organization is a university. We can mention how long the school has been in existence, its structure and diversity, and its areas of distinction. These areas could include such facts as the number of its graduates heading up *Fortune* 500 companies or the number of undergraduates who go on to graduate or professional study. The school could also refer to studies showing how many of its undergraduate, graduate, and professional programs rank nationally.

Perhaps more important than the strength and credibility of the institution it-self, which may be taken for granted, is the reputation of the subdivision actually applying for funds. For example, if Central University has an Institute for the Study and Prevention of Crime, then the grant applicant, who in this case is pre-sumably affiliated with the institute, should highlight the institute's capabilities. How many of Central University's faculty are formally affiliated with the insti-tute? How many grant awards have been made to the institute? Has the institute been diligent in the administration of those grant awards? What services to the community does the institute offer? Has the institute been recognized for its contributions to the field?

Individual Capability: The Curriculum Vitae

A curriculum vitae (CV), the academician's equivalent of a professional rés-umé, is a detailed listing of the person's qualifications. This includes informa-tion such as education, publications, courses taught, grants sought and awarded, and consulting experience. For a research project in criminology or criminal jus-tice, the CV is extremely important because it tells proposal reviewers the extent to which the staff person is qualified to undertake the proposed research.

Although not all CVs are identical, most include several pieces of informa-tion. The following items are listed in no particular order.

Name, Addresses, Telephone Numbers, and E-Mail Addresses

The recipients of the CV must have this information if they are to be able to later make contact. The home address and telephone numbers are optional. Many academic researchers, however, routinely include this information. E-mail addresses are increasingly important, especially for academically based grant applicants. Many professors do not have budgets for long-distance tele-phone calls and thus rely heavily on e-mail for regular communication with colleagues across the country.

Education

For both direct service projects and research projects, relevant education is extremely important. If a member of the proposed project staff must render psy-chotherapy to youthful sex offenders in aftercare, the necessary education must be evident in the education section of the CV.

The education section is the place to list any advanced degrees that the staff members on a grant proposal may have. In general, on CVs, the applicant lists all degrees earned. This should include the college or university that conferred the degree, the year in which the degree was awarded, and the area or field of study in which it was earned.

Other opportunities for this section include any special distinctions or noteworthy accomplishments during the higher education experience. Did the staff member graduate Phi Beta Kappa? Did he or she submit an honors thesis? Was the degree awarded with distinction? Any of these that apply should be highlighted in this section.

Professional Experience

This section generally provides a chronological listing of the positions the staff member has held, as well as the organizations and institutions with which he or she has been affiliated. Usually, the chronology begins with the person's current position and works backward.

Included in these entries are the title of the position, the subdivision in which the person works, and the agency, organization, or institutions of affiliation. The range of dates for each position is also helpful in that it tells how long the staff person served in each position.

It is not uncommon to use this section to mention some details on the nature and level of responsibility for each position. This could include the number of people supervised, the types of projects managed, the extent of travel associated with the positions, and other relevant factors.

Presentations

Criminologists often make presentations in the course of their work. Many belong to scholarly and professional organizations that provide opportunities to present workshops and papers. The appearance of these on the résumé or CV shows professional commitment and interest by the staff. Because published research articles are the primary means of attaining job security and professional recognition, many faculty present their research findings as papers at meetings to refine them. Again, a list of these helps reviewers reading the credentials get a feel for the substantive areas in which the staff person is expert.

Normally, the section of the CV containing presentations has them listed chronologically, beginning with the most recently presented. The entries typically include the author or coauthors, the title of the paper, the name of association holding the meeting, the site of the meeting, and the date of the presentation.

Presentations, therefore, are important to sponsors because they say something about the extent to which the staff participates in professional activities. Although this assessment may not seem fair, the perception is that someone who is involved in the field enough to regularly make presentations may be better qualified to undertake the proposed project.

Publications

Publications are another, more important yardstick by which sponsors and their reviewers measure the capability of staff members. Publications probably are valued more than presentations simply because it is more difficult to get published than it is to present.

Although publications may be the proverbial icing on the cake for staff involved with direct service projects, it is the cake for academicians and researchers. Again, the norms of the academic world suggest that the measure of a researcher's worth is his or her published work. This is true not only for the number of published articles but also for where they appear.

Books and Monographs

If the staff members chosen for our project have authored books or monographs, these should be listed in the CV as well. This section should distinguish who the authors or coauthors are, the title, year of publication, edition, and publisher of the work.

Courses Taught

This section probably has little bearing on the research the applicant wants to pursue, but it is typically found in a CV. It is nothing more than a complete listing of all the courses the individual has taught, including undergraduate, graduate, and professional. It also could include noncredit courses and workshops taught by the individual.

Grants and Contracts

This section is extremely important for the grant seeker. This shows the applicant's grants activity and success to date. The information should include the title of the funded project, the sponsor, the amount of the award, and the date of the award.

Inasmuch as success in grantsmanship builds on itself, the more impressive this section of the CV is, the greater the chances the current request for funding will be looked at favorably. Some applicants also include grants for which they have been turned down. This is a matter of personal preference. Too many unsuccessful attempts documented on the CV may set the wrong tone in the minds of the reviewers.

Honors and Awards

This section gives the individual a chance to brag a bit about his or her distinctions. These may include prizes and awards bestowed by state and national scholarly and professional associations. Distinctions may also consist of teaching awards given by the institution with which the staff member is affiliated. This section may also include directory listings such as *Who's Who.*

OBJECTIVES AND HYPOTHESES FOR A RESEARCH OR AN EVALUATION PROJECT

Although a research or an evaluation project is different from a direct service project, a strong case can be made for developing and committing to specific objectives. One reason is that without objectives, the sponsor may fear that the proposed research will degenerate into a "fishing expedition." This term often is used to describe research that is unfocused or without a strong theoretical basis. By tying the proposed research to specific, testable hypotheses, the applicant brings what otherwise might be a blurry solution into sharper focus.

For example, let's say we are interested in the extent to which narcissistic personality disorder is present in the population of serious, chronic, and violent juvenile offenders. We'll pretend that our review of the literature has revealed that both antisocial and narcissistic personality disorders are more prevalent among confined, youthful offenders than are any of the other psychological disturbances. The literature also says that some of the most violent offenders suffer from narcissistic personality disorder. For the sake of illustration, however, the subject matter is irrelevant because the objectives section relates to milestones of the research project in general.

We will collect the narcissism data on 140 juvenile inmates by September 2000.

Although this objective was contrived for the sake of the example, it illustrates how even research and evaluations can commit to measurable outcomes. The more precise and the more grounded in the theoretical and empirical literature that objectives are, the more they are likely to appeal to those reviewing the grant application or proposal.

9

Revising and Submitting

There are a number of questions that you, the grant seeker, should ask after the draft application or proposal is completed. Most books on grantsmanship simply provide a list of such questions without any rationale or discussion on the consequences. Each of these questions warrants time and space devoted to it. Answering all these questions satisfactorily will strengthen your proposal. Neglecting them will almost certainly weaken it. Use the questions in this chapter as a checklist for all grant applications and proposals.

PROBLEM STATEMENT

Is the problem in the problem statement an important one?

Remember that funding organizations want to help you solve problems in the community. As you read the draft, ask who and how many people will benefit if the project is funded. If the answer suggests that a serious problem plaguing a lot of people will be solved by the project, then you're probably on the right track. Again, enumerate the consequences of not solving the problem. If they have a major impact on an identifiable population, then your problem is probably important.

If pursuing a research project, you need to make sure you haven't overlooked anything in the literature. You don't want to propose a study that's already been done, unless your express purpose is replication. Ask informed colleagues to read the problem statement to make sure it addresses a recognized gap in the professional or scholarly literature.

Keep in mind that although your project may require a personal computer to store program records or analyze data, the absence of such equipment is not your real problem. The computer is merely a tool to use, part of your methods as it were, to help you solve a significant problem. In looking over your problem statement, make sure you haven't inadvertently made you and your professional inconveniences the subject of the request. The absence of computers, office furniture, late-model cruisers, and other staples of criminal justice work is not the real problem. Such items are only tools to help you solve important problems for real people. Go back and perform the consequences exercise in Chapter 2. Perhaps you've overlooked one or more real problems in your community. Propose to solve an important problem for the community, and most likely your convenience needs will be met in the process.

As you read the draft of your application, once again ask yourself what the consequences are if the proposed project does not go forward. If the answer suggests that there will not be any severe consequences, then your problem may not interest most funding organizations.

Have you stated your problem relative to constituents the sponsor will care about?

When you read the draft of your proposal, have you cast yourself or your organization as the primary benefactor? You shouldn't have. Funding organizations want to help you help an important constituent group. In the earlier example of community policing, the community residents are the focus. *They* are in danger of juvenile gangs. It is *their* children who are at risk of becoming involved in delinquent and unruly behavior. It is *their* property values that are decreasing as a result of neighborhood decay. Here, the police department's adoption of community policing is only a vehicle to help the residents in these neighborhoods.

Have you supported your problem statement with appropriate statistics?

Funding organizations want to know how serious your problem is. To help them understand the seriousness of the situation, you need to marshal hard evidence to convince them.

Appropriate statistics are those that speak best to the problem at hand. Did you simply use numbers that were easily available? Or did you seek out those statistics that really paint a vivid, accurate picture of a serious problem?

In preparing the statistics, have you been careful not to inadvertently misrepresent what they say? If you're unsure about the inferences you've drawn from your numbers, ask an informed colleague to see if you're on the right track with what you're reading into the data.

Presentation of data is also important. Everything else being equal, grant reviewers will probably reward the applicant who supplies professionally presented, easy-to-understand graphics.

Make sure you've cited the source(s) of your statistics. Grant reviewers can be a suspicious lot. Some are just curious. Some may even want to check out the numbers for themselves. Let them know exactly where these numbers came from.

METHODS

Have you made clear what you intend to do to solve the problem?

As professionals, we sometimes take for granted that everyone knows the processes and terminology of criminal justice. This simply isn't true. It well may not be true of those who will be reading the application or proposal. In reading over the draft version of your proposal, make sure you've laid out the entire solution you're proposing from beginning to end. Make sure you've answered all those questions the methods section is supposed to answer for the proposal reviewer. Don't make the assumption that the reader will fill in the blanks. If there is anything missing in the description of the solution, now is the time to put it in.

Have you shown the role of staff in undertaking the solution?

This is the *who* question. Although you don't want to go into the qualifications of those who will be implementing the solution to your problem, you do want to imply that staff of some sort will be employing the methods discussed. People interview victims. They investigate criminal cases. They collect and analyze data. Show in the methods sections how staff will be involved in undertaking the solution to the problem. In our community policing example, those responsible for the solution most likely will be law enforcement officers. Show their role in implementing the solution to the problem.

Our hypothetical restorative justice project had an investigator and a restoration counselor. It is important to make sure their roles are clear. Who will be doing the investigating? How will they perform their duties? Will they request periodic records checks at the local law enforcement agency? Will they also request these of the state's Criminal Identification Bureau? Grant reviewers will expect these types of details to see exactly how the proposed project will address the problem.

Have you discussed those affected by the problem and its solution?

Many grant applications require you to discuss the population at whom your solution is directed. Have you described this population? Have you differentiated them from similar groups you don't intend to serve with your project?

Have you defined the variables and values?

If when reading the draft of your research or evaluation proposal, you find you always refer to data without ever being specific, you've probably paid insufficient attention to specifics. Bear in mind that the reviewers of your research proposal will likely be researchers themselves. Consequently, they will expect the level of detail they are used to putting into their own proposals for research projects.

In the case of the research project, think data definition, collection, and analysis. Where are the data going to come from? Will they be primary or secondary? What are the variable names, their values, and levels of measurement?

Have you spelled out exactly how you are going to analyze the data?

If in the haste of drafting your proposal, you committed to "using appropriate univariate and multivariate statistical techniques," now is the time to flesh out such a skeletal phrase. Reviewers are going to expect specificity. Have you walked the reader through precisely how you will analyze your data? Instead of generalities such as "appropriate multivariate techniques," make sure you've committed to using logistic regression, if that's indeed appropriate for the type of data you intend to collect.

Even if you omitted the specifics of techniques for the sake of finishing the draft, please pay attention to them in the rewrite. If you don't know whether it's appropriate to perform an orthogonal or oblique rotation on your factor-analyzed data, consult an expert who can give you the right answer. People in the research community of criminology and criminal justice routinely help each other by reading drafts of grant proposals. Take advantage of others' expertise. Most important, assume that those reviewing your application or proposal will be experts in their respective field. Show them you've done your homework, and you'll be rewarded.

OBJECTIVES AND MEASUREMENT

Are your objectives measurable?

Test your objectives by checking to see if the verbiage suggests some sort of change. Funding organizations want to know that the solution they're paying for is making some demonstrable change in the problem.

Are your objectives reasonable?

If our hypothetical prosecutor commits to a 100% reduction in recidivism among his diversion clients, he undoubtedly will arouse great suspicion in those reading the proposal. On the other hand, few eyebrows will rise if a 10% reduction is the objective because it seems more reasonable. In looking over your draft application, make sure you haven't reached too high or too low in creating measurable indicators of what you hope to achieve. Few sponsors expect perfect results, but most may expect grantees to at least come close to what they've committed to in the proposal.

Does your proposal have an evaluation plan?

If your proposed project does not have a formal evaluation plan, will there be at least some effort to measure the extent to which you have achieved your objectives? If you do have an evaluation plan, will the evaluation be performed by your organization's staff? If so, how will you counteract the possible criticism that your results may not be objective?

BUDGET

Have you requested only what is necessary?

The methods section of the application at least implies personnel, equipment, travel, and other project necessities. It is in the budget that you have to specifically ask for those necessities without which the proposed solution cannot go forward. If a new staff person is necessary, make sure you've included the position in the budget. And don't forget related services such as secretarial support.

The flip side of this question has to do with those things that are not true necessities. Sometimes, some grant seekers, especially those of us who routinely write lots of grant proposals, can be guilty of including a stock list of budget categories instead of justifying each item. A careful, critical reading of the draft application will help you reexamine what's necessary and what may be frivolous.

Has all equipment been adequately justified?

Grant applicants are often tempted to request computers in their proposals. This is understandable, given their importance in society in general these days. But it's not the funding organization's obligation to make sure you're on-line. A computer should be in the project only if it's indispensable to carrying out the solution to the problem. If an existing computer can be used for the project's purposes without causing problems, keep the computer request out. If it's necessary, both the methods section and the budget narrative should reveal exactly how the computer will support the proposed solution. Reviewers will likely scrutinize any such request, so be sure it's well justified.

Are the travel expenses adequately justified?

As mentioned earlier, a common, albeit understandable, trait of human nature is the desire to periodically get out of the office. Again, when we are drafting grant applications, the light goes on: "We can go to that conference in Palm Springs now, after all." Almost all of us succumb to the lure of going to exciting places, especially if the trip promises more inviting weather than what we would face otherwise. So why not tuck the trip into the grant proposal? After all, the conference is somewhat work related, right?

The reason not to put unnecessary trips in a grant application is that grant reviewers frown on such things. It's not that they can't identify with the longing for time away from the office. It's not that they, too, don't enjoy warm, tropical climates when the snow is falling. The real reason is that if the grant reviewers take their jobs seriously, they have to insist that you justify the travel relative to the problem detailed in the problem statement. The travel, including that involving conferences and workshops, must be related to the problem in the problem statement and to the solution detailed in the methods section. If your diversion coordinator has to attend a seminar on diversion in San Francisco because it's the only one offered and she needs the training to perform her duties competently, include it in the budget. On the other hand, if there is training available locally, or if your coordinator already knows the diversion business inside and out, don't be greedy and opt for the meeting just because you think the sponsor will pay for it. If the trip looks frivolous, cut it out of the project. Poorly justified trips that look like junkets are red flags to reviewers. Red flags mean lower scores. Lower scores translate into poorer chances of getting funded.

Have you eliminated any and all computation errors?

When drafting grant proposals, it is extremely easy to make arithmetic mistakes. Often, this is a function of the involvement of several people who, racing against an impending deadline, make change after change to the budget. Still, in the final revision stage, you must carefully go over each set of figures to make sure the calculations are correct. Again, if numbers are not your strong suit, find someone who can competently find and correct any mistakes.

INDIVIDUAL AND ORGANIZATIONAL CAPABILITIES

Have you shown the applicant organization to be credible?

Often, during the draft stage, you may give short shrift to the organization. If you expect a funding organization to take a chance on your agency, what message do you have to convey? The answer is integrity, financial stability, competence, and other such positives.

Are the staff members qualified to undertake the proposed project?

In your haste to assemble your draft, you may have simply pulled a few facts from the staff résumés or curricula vitae. Do those facts support that the staff members are suitably qualified to undertake the solution to the problem? Let's take our example of the prosecutor's diversion program. Does the diversion coordinator have the skills necessary to work with these first-time offenders? Can she identify their employment, substance abuse treatment, and other needs? Is she familiar with available social services that may improve her clients' adjustment?

If the staff for the proposed project are yet to be hired, have you provided enough detail on qualifications you believe are relevant to conducting the proposed project? You often do not know who will be staffing your project, but you should know what set of qualifications such an individual will have to hold to meet your standards.

WRITING PROBLEMS

Have you employed a simple, direct writing style?

When you reread your draft, break up any sentences that are too long. On the other hand, you may be guilty of too many short, choppy sentences in a row. Remember that readers like variation in sentence length and type. If you have a grammar-checking program, you are well advised to analyze your prose for these problems. In the absence of such electronic assistance, a competent grammarian should be able to accomplish the same job.

Have you avoided the use of passive voice?

For those of you who have access to a grammar-check program on your computers, this is another reason to use it. Grammar check by computer should not be a substitute for a thorough reading of the draft proposal for grammatical errors. But programs such as Grammatik are based on sound rules of grammar and use.

They can help you weed out passive voice created during a hasty drafting process. Although the use of passive voice is not a fatal flaw, why not present your case for funding in the most straightforward and understandable manner possible?

Have you minimized the use of adjectives and adverbs?

Excessive modifiers clutter up sentences. They usually fail to prop up the nouns and verbs they modify. Get rid of all you can. The result will be a cleaner, crisper style that doesn't bog the reader down.

Have you been repetitive?

If you have something important to say, say it only once. Repeating yourself only annoys readers. Have your editor or proofreader pay special attention to this writing problem.

Have you avoided jargon and unnecessarily big words?

As indicated earlier, the point in preparing a grant application is to convey a serious problem. To do so, you first need to make yourself understood. Keeping criminal justice jargon to a minimum is one way to do this. Another is to avoid the multisyllabic, Latin-based words that send readers to the dictionary. Your aim is to make the funding organization understand your problem and proposed solution, not to impress with polysyllabic words.

Are all the words, including names, spelled correctly?

Criminal justice professionals, perhaps like everyone else, like to see the names in their field spelled correctly. Although this isn't a fatal flaw in a grant application, instances of misspelling irritate reviewers. It should go without saying that you don't ever want to irritate reviewers.

APPLICATION REQUIREMENTS

Does your application have all the necessary forms?

Federal grant applications in the United States invariably come with a series of forms that must be completed. One such form is the Standard 424 sheet, which serves as a face sheet for all such applications for funding. Other forms include assurances about such matters as drug-free workplace, equal employment opportunity commitment, and debarment. These forms are not optional. Each must be part of the packet. Be sure that all the forms and application sections are submitted in the specified order. Check also to ensure that the forms bear the necessary signatures from the appropriate authorities. Don't wait until the last minute to get these necessary signatures, in case the designated official is unavailable.

Does your application or proposal have all the necessary sections?

In the haste to complete a grant application, it is common to leave out a section. This tends to be more of a problem when several people are working on the proposal at once. It is wise to develop a checklist of every necessary form and section of the proposal. Use this checklist before the photocopies are printed and collated.

Have you abided by length requirements?

Some funding organizations give applicants a page limit for concept papers and proposals. Some also instruct their grant reviewers not to read pages beyond the specified limit. Therefore, know what the limitations are and abide by them. It is also wise not to try to circumvent page limitations through the use of smaller fonts. The funding organizations are on to that trick.

Has the application or proposal been properly collated?

This seems like a no-brainer, but at least some applicants invariably shuffle sections of their submissions before they mail them. Again, a checklist will help prevent this sort of problem.

Have you made the required number of copies?

Most funding organizations have more than one person reviewing the proposal. The point in asking you to submit x number of copies is to save themselves the expense and bother. They wouldn't ask for these copies if they didn't really need them. Make sure you've included an original and the appropriate number of copies before you seal the package.

Do you know exactly when the application or proposal is due?

Some grant deadlines center on when the application is received. For others, the deadline is determined by the postmark. Some deadlines specify a time in addition to the date beyond which applications will not be considered. Double-check the precise means and time by which the proposal must be submitted. Allow sufficient mailing time for the grant packet to reach its destination by the deadline.

10

Sources of Grants
and Grant Information

There are literally hundreds of grant-making organizations. Those listed in this section, however, are of special interest to grant seekers in criminal justice and criminology. As with other facets of grantsmanship, the reader is encouraged not to stop here. There are yet other agencies and organizations not listed that may well offer support for the reader's area of interest.

FEDERAL AGENCIES

National Institute of Justice

The National Institute of Justice (NIJ), the research and development arm of the U.S. Department of Justice, undertakes and sponsors a variety of initiatives to control crime and address problems of the criminal justice system. It is one of several funding agencies that make up the Office of Justice Programs. Through the most recent crime control legislation, the NIJ is committed to fulfilling its mission by

- Conducting national demonstration projects that employ innovative or promising approaches for improving criminal justice
- Developing new technologies to fight crime and improve criminal justice
- Evaluating the effectiveness of criminal justice programs and identifying programs that promise to be successful if continued or repeated
- Recommending actions that can be taken by federal, state, and local governments as well as private organizations to improve criminal justice

- Carrying out research on criminal behavior
- Developing new methods of crime prevention and reduction of crime and delinquency

As of this writing, the topics covered by NIJ include

- Corrections
- Courts
- Crime prevention
- Criminal justice statistics
- Drugs and crime
- International issues
- Justice grants
- Juvenile justice
- Law enforcement
- Other criminal justice resources
- Research and evaluation
- Victims

The NIJ has come up with four criteria that are most important in its decision-making process. It is wise for all grant applicants to keep these in mind for projects submitted to other agencies as well.

1. Impact of the proposed project
2. Feasibility of the approach to the issue, including technical merit and practical considerations
3. Originality of the approach, including creativity of the proposal and capability of the research staff
4. Economy of the approach (Applicants bear the responsibility of demonstrating to the panel that the proposed study addresses the critical issues of the topic area and that the study findings could ultimately contribute to a practical application in law enforcement or criminal justice. Reviewers will assess applicants' awareness of related research and studies and their ability to direct the research or study toward answering questions of policy or improving the state of criminal justice operations.)

The NIJ can be contacted at

National Institute of Justice
810 Seventh Street, NW
Washington, DC 20531
Phone: (202) 307-2942
Fax: (202) 307-6394
WWW: http://www.ncjrs.org/

Office of Juvenile Justice and Delinquency Prevention

The Office of Juvenile Justice and Delinquency Prevention (OJJDP) is another funding arm of the Office of Justice Programs within the U.S. Department of Justice. As its name implies, it is focused primarily on awarding formula and discretionary grants for purposes related to youth crime and juvenile justice processing. The formula grants are awarded to states and territories; the discretionary grants are made by OJJDP.

Some of the recent funding opportunities within OJJDP include

- Evaluation of Youth Substance Use Prevention Program
- Training and Technical Assistance for National Innovations to Reduce Disproportionate Minority Confinement (The Deborah Ann Wysinger Memorial Program)
- Youth Substance Use Prevention Program
- Missing and Exploited Children's Program

The OJJDP can be contacted at

Office of Juvenile Justice and Delinquency Prevention
810 Seventh Street, NW
Washington, DC 20531
Phone: (202) 307-5911
WWW: http://ojjdp.ncjrs.org/

Office for Victims of Crime

The Office for Victims of Crime (OVC) is set up to serve those who have been victimized by violent and serious crime. In addition to the many victim assistance programs it supports across the nation, it also provides victim compensation funds for those who have been victimized by violent and other serious crimes.

The OVC can be contacted at

Office for Victims of Crime
810 Seventh Street, NW
Washington, DC 20531
Phone: (800) 627-6872
WWW: http://www.ojp.usdoj.gov/ovc/

Bureau of Justice Assistance

The Bureau of Justice Assistance (BJA), a component of the Office of Justice Programs, U.S. Department of Justice, supports innovative programs that strengthen the nation's criminal justice system by assisting state and local governments in combating violent crime and drug abuse.

The BJA meets its mission by offering

- Funding
- Evaluation
- Training
- Technical assistance
- Information support to state and community criminal justice programs, thus effectively forming partnerships with state and local jurisdictions

The BJA supports criminal justice both nationally and in the states and territories through the Edward Byrne Memorial State and Local Law Enforcement Assistance Program. This includes both formula grants to states and territories and discretionary grants to public and private agencies and private nonprofit organizations. The wide range of opportunities available through the Byrne formula grants program may offer funding for the following:

- Personnel
- Equipment and training
- Technical assistance
- Innovative programs
- Information systems
- Prosecution
- Rehabilitation of criminals
- Victim programming

Applicants interested in applying for Byrne grants should consult the list of state administering agencies (SAAs) in Appendix B. The BJA also has a discretionary grants program. For this program, applicants apply directly to the BJA, generally in response to a solicitation that appears in the *Federal Register.* Notices are also routinely sent to criminal justice constituents on its mailing list. The discretionary program recently has offered funding opportunities emphasizing

- Educational and training programs for criminal justice personnel
- Technical assistance to state and local units of government
- Projects that are national or multijurisdictional in scope
- Financial assistance for demonstration programs that, in view of previous research or experience, are likely to be successful in more than one jurisdiction

For more information about the BJA, contact

Bureau of Justice Assistance
810 Seventh Street, NW
Washington, DC 20531
Phone: (800) 688-4252
WWW: http://www.ojp.usdoj.gov/bja

Violence Against Women Grants Office

The Violence Against Women Grants Office (VAWGO) administers both formula and discretionary grant programs, most recently those authorized by the Violence Against Women Act of 1994. The program assists the nation's criminal justice system in responding to the needs and concerns of women who have been, or potentially could be, victimized by violence. The grant programs target three principal groups: law enforcement, prosecution, and victim services professionals.

The VAWGO can be contacted at

Violence Against Women Grants Office
810 Seventh Street, NW
Washington, DC 20531
Phone: (202) 307-6026
Fax: (202) 305-2589
E-mail: askocpa@ojp.usdoj.gov
WWW: http://www.ojp.usdoj.gov/vawgo/

Corrections Program Office

The Corrections Program Office (CPO), another division of the Office of Justice Programs within the U.S. Department of Justice, administers grant programs of interest to corrections professionals. The CPO can be contacted at

Corrections Program Office
810 Seventh Street, NW, 6th Floor
Washington, DC 20531
Phone: (800) 848-6325 or (202) 305-4866
Fax: (202) 307-2019
E-mail: askcpo@ojp.usdoj.gov
WWW: http://www.ojp.usdoj.gov/cpo/

State Justice Institute

The State Justice Institute (SJI) awards grants to improve the quality of justice in state courts. Through the years, the SJI has funded more than 1,000 projects totaling more than $100 million. Grant seekers should also obtain a copy of the SJI booklet of grant-writing tips.

The SJI can be contacted at

State Justice Institute
1650 King Street, Suite 600
Alexandria, VA 22314
Phone: (703) 684-6100
Fax: (703) 684-7618
E-mail: SJI@clark.net

National Science Foundation

The National Science Foundation (NSF) is a federal agency that funds scientific research. The NSF is relevant to criminology and criminal justice because it funds research under the umbrella term "law and society." Prospective applicants should contact the agency for examples of recently funded projects in social control, crime causation, violence, deterrence, and other areas of interest to criminal justice researchers.

The NSF will consider proposals from the following types of applicants. The NSF also funds dissertation research in its areas of interest.

● Universities and colleges
● Nonprofit, nonacademic organizations
● For-profit organizations
● State and local governments
● Unaffiliated individuals

The NSF can be contacted at

National Science Foundation
4201 Wilson Blvd.
Arlington, VA 22230
Phone: (703) 306-1234
WWW: http://www.nsf.gov

Centers for Disease Control and Prevention

As the title implies, the Centers for Disease Control and Prevention (CDC) are concerned with the prevention and control of diseases, including intentional injury. This has led to the CDC's ambitious program of research and grant making to understand and control violent crime.

The CDC can be contacted at

Centers for Disease Control and Prevention
1600 Clifton Road, NE
Atlanta, GA 30333
Phone: (404) 639-3311
E-mail: netinfo@cdc.gov
WWW: http://www.cdc.gov/

SOURCES OF PRIVATE FUNDS

A number of private foundations have shown an interest in funding projects that promise to prevent or control crime or delinquency or to improve the administration of criminal or juvenile justice. Relatively few practitioners or academicians in criminal justice regularly approach large, private foundations for support. Although their purpose areas are often narrow, and the competition for their dollars is keen, private sources remain an avenue for those in criminology and criminal justice.

Although the following list is not all-inclusive, it illustrates that private foundations do, in fact, support research and service projects of interest to those in criminal justice and criminology. Those pursuing private sources of support should check reference sources such as those published by the Foundation Center for additional foundations that may be relevant to their search for grant funds.

Readers are cautioned not to apply to any foundation for funding until they have made a preliminary inquiry to see if there is a match between the problem they want to solve and the interests of these foundations. Most private foundations, including those listed here, have a preferred method of making such inquiries. A phone call or a visit to their home pages should provide this information.

Annie E. Casey Foundation

The Annie E. Casey Foundation supports programs that assist disadvantaged youths. Specifically, the foundation is interested in helping children and families in innovative ways that are also cost-effective. The foundation can be contacted at

Annie E. Casey Foundation
701 St. Paul Street
Baltimore, MD 21202
Phone: (410) 547-6600
Fax: (410) 547-6624
E-mail: webmail@aecf.org
WWW: http://www.aecf.org/

Center on Crime, Communities & Culture

Philanthropist George Soros began this center to improve the criminal justice system's understanding of, and approach to, crime, criminals, and victims. To that end, the foundation has funded demonstration projects, research and evaluation studies, and fellowships. Of special interest are criminal justice programs that are outstanding and innovative, including the following that received center funding:

- $150,000 to the American Civil Liberties Union, Washington, D.C., for support of the National Prison Project
- $119,000 to the Boys and Girls Club of Chicago, for a multidisciplinary approach to violence prevention for youth victims of violence
- $75,000 in renewal funds to the Center on Juvenile and Criminal Justice, Washington, D.C., to support research and media advocacy to promote a progressive criminal justice agenda
- $150,000 to Free at Last, East Palo Alto, California, for a community justice initiative to end systematic drug-related incarceration in East Palo Alto, California
- $44,000 in renewal support to the Summit County Sheriff's Office, Akron, Ohio, for a psychiatry training program in a local jail

The center, which has a distinguished advisory board, can be contacted at

Center on Crime, Communities & Culture
400 West 59th Street
New York, NY 10019
Phone: (212) 548-0135
Fax: (212) 548-4677
E-mail: cccc@sorosny.org
WWW: http://www.soros.org/crime/

Edna McConnell Clark Foundation

The Edna McConnell Clark Foundation is committed to improving conditions for those in poor and disadvantaged communities, especially children and families. The foundation is interested in projects that have been unable to secure adequate support from other sources. Noteworthy among their initiatives is the Program for Children. This should be of interest to those working in the allied justice fields because it is designed to protect children from abuse and neglect.

For additional information, contact

> The Edna McConnell Clark Foundation
> 250 Park Avenue
> New York, NY 10177-0026

Do Right Foundation

The philanthropic work of the Do Right Foundation is grounded in the philosophy of Dr. W. Edwards Deming, who became famous for developing and espousing quality management. The foundation is interested in promoting this philosophy by starting small pilot programs that, if found to be successful, can be expanded later.

Of interest to the Do Right Foundation are the reduction of violent crime, fighting joblessness, increasing the productivity of our legal system, and developing an ever-improving generation of children.

The Do Right Foundation can be contacted at

> Do Right Foundation
> 852 5th Avenue, Suite 215
> San Diego, CA 92101
> Phone: (619) 235-5634
> Fax: (619) 233-6134
> E-mail: lisat@adnc.com
> WWW: http://www.doright.org/

Robert Wood Johnson Foundation

The Robert Wood Johnson Foundation was founded through the bequest of the man who built the Johnson & Johnson health care empire. In 1996, the foundation awarded $267 million in grants.

The Robert Wood Johnson Foundation is committed to offering support in the following areas:

- Demonstrations
- Gathering and monitoring health-related statistics
- Training and fellowship programs
- Policy analysis
- Health services research
- Technical assistance
- Public education
- Communications
- Evaluation

As those working in criminal justice and criminology well know, violence has become one of the biggest public health problems in the United States. Substance abuse also affects the health of criminal justice populations. Readers are encouraged to check for a match between their problem and the funding interests of the Johnson Foundation. As with all major private foundations, the prospective applicant should be forewarned that competition for funding is keen.

The foundation may be contacted at

The Robert Wood Johnson Foundation
P.O. Box 2316
Route 1 and College Road East
Princeton, NJ 08543-2316
Phone: (609) 452-8701
E-mail: mail@rwjf.org
WWW: http://www.rwjf.org/

Henry Luce Foundation, Inc.

The Henry Luce Foundation is interested in public policy issues, including those related to criminal justice. In the past, it has supported studies on the jury system. Recently, the Luce Foundation has funded several projects addressing at-risk youths.

The Luce Foundation can be contacted at

The Henry Luce Foundation, Inc.
111 West 50th Street
New York, NY 10020
Phone: (212) 489-7700
Fax: (212) 581-9541
WWW: http://www.hluce.org/

John D. and Catherine T. MacArthur Foundation

The MacArthur Foundation has a considerable history of supporting projects of interest to those in criminology and criminal justice. One of the most notable is the Project on Human Development in Chicago's Neighborhoods. This multi-year, multilayer study may turn out to be the definitive study on crime causation. Using an accelerated longitudinal design, the study will cover eight overlapping cohorts, allowing researchers to follow the paths of criminal careers in an abbreviated period.

The interested grant seeker may contact the MacArthur Foundation at

John D. and Catherine T. MacArthur Foundation
140 South Dearborn Street, Suite 1100
Chicago, IL 60603-5285
Phone: (312) 726-8000
E-mail: 4answers@macfdn.org
WWW: http://www.macfdn.org/

STATE AGENCIES

State Administering Agencies

Many of the states and territories have what became known as state criminal justice planning agencies, which the federal Bureau of Justice Assistance now refers to as state administering agencies (SAAs). Most of the SAAs came into being in the late 1960s and early 1970s as a result of the Omnibus Crime Control and Safe Streets Act of 1968. After President Johnson's Commission on Law Enforcement and the Administration of Justice made its recommendations, the 1968 Crime Control Act pumped millions of dollars into the states. The states needed a bureaucracy to oversee these monies, and thus the SAAs were born. These agencies generally perform a number of functions including grant administration, criminal justice information system oversight, policy development, and others.

The grant administration function of SAAs makes these agencies an extremely important source of funds for those working in criminal justice. As a source of grant funds, the SAAs are especially attractive because applicants most often have to compete only with others from the same state. Although competition is still keen, this smaller pool of applicants increases the chances for an award.

Another factor that increases the odds of receiving an award is the absence of true peer review. As mentioned above, some federal agencies such as the NIJ and the NSF use professionals from outside their organizations to help review proposals.

The grant programs administered by SAAs offer numerous opportunities for those in criminal justice. For example, the Edward Byrne Memorial State and Local Law Enforcement Assistance Program, administered federally by the Bureau of Justice Assistance, has program categories covering topics ranging from multijurisdictional law enforcement task forces to community-based correctional programming.

Other potential state-level sources of grant support include

- Offices of the Attorney General
- Departments of Mental Health
- Drug Control Offices
- Departments of Youth Services
- Departments of Corrections
- Departments of Education
- Departments of Public Safety
- Departments of Alcohol and Drug Addiction Services

Those interested in what these various agencies have to offer should contact them and request to be placed on their mailing lists. Many, if not most, of these state agencies now have World Wide Web home pages that detail their services, including grant programs.

INFORMATION SOURCES

Grant seekers should be familiar with several sources of information on grants. Again, the following list of sources is not exhaustive, but it contains the sources that offer the information that grant seekers need to know most.

Federal Register

Published by the U.S. government every weekday except holidays, the *Federal Register* contains notices of funding opportunities, including grants and cooperative agreements. Subscriptions to the *Federal Register* are expensive, and small criminal justice agencies may find it difficult or impossible to justify the cost; nevertheless, access to the information it contains is critical for the criminal justice grant seeker.

Catalog of Federal Domestic Assistance

This huge catalog contains a description of every grant program offered by the U.S. government. Although it's not a resource that most grant seekers would need to consult daily, leafing through it gives the reader a feel for the many grant opportunities available at the federal level. It also contains the catalog numbers that must be present on federal grant applications to identify the precise program applied for.

Most grant seekers will not want to purchase the catalog. Because many libraries will have a copy, it makes more sense to use one there.

The Foundation Directory

The Foundation Directory, a rather hefty volume published by the Foundation Center in New York, offers detailed information about private foundations having assets greater than $2 million or distributing $200,000 or more annually. In addition to listing the foundation's giving priorities, which is crucial for the criminal justice grant seeker to know, the Foundation Directory also includes the foundation's address, contact person, date of establishment, donors, financial data, purpose and activities, fields of interest, types of support, application information, and recent grants.

This is another book that most criminal justice grant seekers will want to use in the library. Persons wishing to purchase a copy should contact the Foundation Center at the address and phone number listed at the end of this chapter.

Criminal Justice Funding Report

A biweekly publication, the *Criminal Justice Funding Report* contains information on both federal and private grants of interest to criminal justice professionals. In addition to detailed data on criminal justice funding opportunities, the report also features "Policy News" and a "Legislative Update."

One word of caution about newsletters as sources of grants information: Seldom, if at all, can a newsletter transmit grants information to potential applicants as quickly as do the *Federal Register* and the Internet. Although these newsletters contain useful information, in many cases applicants already have lost valuable time by the time they learn of the funding opportunity.

Those interested in subscribing to the *Criminal Justice Funding Report* may contact

Capitol City Publishers
3030 Clarendon Blvd., Suite 219
Arlington, VA 22201
Phone: (703) 525-3080
Fax: (703) 525-3044
E-mail: fitz@mail.wdn.com

The Foundation Center

A valuable source of funding information, the Foundation Center is a nonprofit organization that was established in 1956 to assist grant-awarding organizations and grant seekers by making available a wide variety of material on private grants. The Foundation Center meets its mission by providing a number of useful reference works on foundations and related matters. Its home page offers links to a number of private foundations and permits the grant seeker to search for relevant foundations by subject or geography.

Those interested in learning more about the center can do so by contacting

The Foundation Center
79 Fifth Avenue/16th Street
New York, NY 10003-3076
Phone: (212) 620-4230 or (800) 424-9836
Fax: (212) 807-3677
E-mail: library@fdncenter.org
WWW: http://fdncenter.org

Appendix A

Statistical Analysis Centers

SACs, as discussed earlier in this book, are rich sources of statewide criminal justice data. They also conduct various studies that may be relevant to the grant seeker's problem. Because the centers receive federal support, they are accustomed to fielding requests for information.

Alabama

Statistical Analysis Center
Alabama Criminal Justice
    Information Center
770 Washington Avenue, Suite 350
Montgomery, AL 36130
Phone: (334) 242-4900
Fax: (334) 242-0577

Alaska

Statistical Analysis Center
Justice Center
University of Alaska, Anchorage
3211 Providence Drive
Anchorage, AK 99508
Phone: (907) 786-1810
Fax: (907) 786-7777
WWW: http://www.uaa.alaska.edu/just/

Arizona

Statistical Analysis Center
Arizona Criminal Justice Commission
1501 West Washington, Suite 207
Phoenix, AZ 85007
Phone: (602) 542-1928
Fax: (602) 542-4852

Arkansas

Arkansas Crime Information Center
One Capitol Mall
Little Rock, AR 72201
Phone: (501) 682-2222
Fax: (501) 682-7444
WWW: http://www.acic.org

California

Statistical Analysis Center
California Department of Justice
P.O. Box 903427

Sacramento, CA 94203
Phone: (916) 227-3282
Fax: (916) 227-0427
WWW: http://caag.state.ca.us

Colorado

Office of Research and Statistics
Colorado Division of Criminal Justice
700 Kipling Street, Suite 3000
Denver, CO 80403
Phone: (303) 239-4453
Fax: (303) 239-4491
WWW: http://www.state.co.us/gov_dir/
  cdps/dcj/dcj.htm

Connecticut

Office of Policy and Development
Policy Development and
  Planning Division
450 Capitol Avenue, Mail Stop 52-CPD
P.O. Box 341441
Hartford, CT 06134
Phone: (860) 418-6376
Fax: (860) 418-6496
WWW: http://www.state.ct.us/opm/pdpd/
  justice/sac.htm

Delaware

Delaware Statistical Analysis Center
60 The Plaza
Dover, DE 19901
Phone: (302) 739-4626
Fax: (302) 739-4630

District of Columbia

Office of Grants Management
  and Development
717 14th Street, NW, Suite 400
Washington, DC 20005
Phone: (202) 727-6537
Fax: (202) 727-1617

Florida

Statistical Analysis Center
Florida Department of Law Enforcement
2331 Phillips Road
Tallahassee, FL 32308
Phone: (904) 487-4808

Fax: (904) 487-4812
WWW: http://www.fdle.state.fl.us/FSAC

Georgia

Statistical Analysis Center
Georgia Criminal Justice
  Coordinating Council
503 Oak Place, Suite 540
Atlanta, GA 30349
Phone: (404) 559-4949
Fax: (404) 559-4960

Hawaii

Research and Statistics
Department of the Attorney General
Crime Prevention and
  Justice Assistance Division
425 Queen Street
Honolulu, HI 96813
Phone: (808) 586-1420
Fax: (808) 586-1373
WWW: http://www.cpja.ag.state.hi.us

Idaho

Statistical Analysis Center
Idaho Department of Law Enforcement
P.O. Box 700
Meridian, ID 83630
Phone: (208) 884-7044
Fax: (208) 884-7094

Illinois

Illinois Criminal Justice
  Information Authority
120 South Riverside Plaza, Suite 1016
Chicago, IL 60606
Phone: (312) 793-8550
Fax: (312) 793-8422
WWW: http://www.icjia.org

Indiana

Statistical Analysis Center
Indiana Criminal Justice Institute
302 West Washington Street,
  Room E-209
Indianapolis, IN 46204
Phone: (317) 232-7611
Fax: (317) 232-4979

Iowa

Statistical Analysis Center
Criminal and Juvenile Justice Planning
Lucas State Office Building
Des Moines, IA 50319
Phone: (515) 242-5816
Fax: (515) 242-6119

Kansas

Criminal Justice Coordinating Council
Kansas Sentencing Commission
700 Southwest Jackson, Suite 501
Topeka, KS 66603
Phone: (913) 296-0923
Fax: (913) 296-0927

Kentucky

Statistical Analysis Center
Office of the Attorney General
700 Capitol Avenue, Suite 116
Frankfort, KY 40602-3449
Phone: (502) 696-5300
Fax: (502) 564-8310

Louisiana

Statistical Analysis Center
Louisiana Commission on
   Law Enforcement
1885 Wooddale Boulevard, Suite 708
Baton Rouge, LA 70806
Phone: (504) 925-4429
Fax: (504) 925-6752

Maine

Statistical Analysis Center
Department of Corrections
State of Maine
State House Station #111
Augusta, ME 04333-0111
Phone: (207) 287-4386
Fax: (207) 287-4370

Maryland

Maryland Justice Analysis Center
University of Maryland
2220 LeFrak Hall
College Park, MD 20742

Phone: (301) 405-4701
Fax: (301) 314-0179

Massachusetts

Research and Evaluation
Executive Office of Public Safety
Programs Division
100 Cambridge Street, Room 2100
Boston, MA 02202
Phone: (617) 727-6300, ext. 325
Fax: (617) 727-5356

Michigan

Michigan Justice Statistics Center
School of Criminal Justice
Michigan State University
560 Baker Hall
East Lansing, MI 48824
Phone: (517) 353-4515
Fax: (517) 432-1787
WWW: http://www.ssc.msu.edu/~cj

Minnesota

Criminal Justice Center
Minnesota Planning
658 Cedar Street
St. Paul, MN 55155
Phone: (612) 297-3279
Fax: (612) 296-3698
WWW: http://www.mnplan.state.mn.us

Missouri

Statistical Analysis Center
Missouri State Highway Patrol
1510 East Elm Street
P.O. Box 568
Jefferson City, MO 65102
Phone: (573) 526-6299
Fax: (573) 526-6274

Montana

Statistical Analysis Center
Montana Board of Crime Control
303 North Roberts Street
Helena, MT 59620
Phone: (406) 444-4298
Fax: (406) 444-4722

Nebraska

Statistical Analysis Center
Nebraska Commission on Law
  Enforcement and Criminal Justice
P.O. Box 94946
Lincoln, NE 68509
Phone: (402) 471-2194
Fax: (402) 471-2837

New Hampshire

Department of Justice
Office of the Attorney General
State House Annex
33 Capitol Street
Concord, NH 03301
Phone: (603) 271-1234
Fax: (603) 271-2110

New Jersey

Research and Evaluation Section
Division of Criminal Justice
25 Market Street, CN 085
Trenton, NJ 08625
Phone: (609) 984-5693
Fax: (609) 984-4473

New Mexico

Statistical Analysis Center
University of New Mexico
Institute for Social Research
2808 Central, SE
Albuquerque, NM 87106
Phone: (505) 277-4257
Fax: (505) 277-4215
WWW: http://www.unm.edu/~isrnet/
  SAC.html

New York

Bureau of Statistical Services
NYS Division of Criminal
  Justice Services
Executive Park Tower
Stuyvesant Plaza
Albany, NY 12203-3764
Phone: (518) 457-8381
Fax: (518) 485-8039
WWW: http://criminaljustice.state.ny.us

North Carolina

North Carolina Governor's
  Crime Commission
Criminal Justice Analysis Center
3824 Barrett Drive, Suite 100
Raleigh, NC 27609
Phone: (919) 571-4736
Fax: (919) 571-4745
WWW: http://www.gcc.state.nc.us

North Dakota

Information Services Section
Bureau of Criminal Investigation
P.O. Box 1054
Bismarck, ND 58502
Phone: (701) 328-5500
Fax: (701) 328-5510

Northern Mariana Islands

Criminal Justice Planning Agency
Commonwealth of the Northern
  Mariana Islands
P.O. Box 1133-CK
Saipan, MP 96950
Phone: (670) 664-4550
Fax: (670) 664-4560
WWW: http://www.saipan.com/
gov/branches/cjpa

Ohio

Office of Criminal Justice Services
400 East Town Street, Suite 120
Columbus, OH 43215-4242
Phone: (614) 466-5174
Fax: (614) 466-0308
WWW: http://www.ocjs.state.oh.us

Oklahoma

Oklahoma Statistical Analysis Center
5500 North Western, Suite 245
Oklahoma City, OK 73118
Phone: (405) 858-7025
Fax: (405) 858-7040
WWW: http://www.state.ok.us/~ocjrc

Oregon

Mr. Phillip Lemman
Executive Director

Oregon Criminal Justice Commission
155 Cottage Street, NE
Salem, OR 97310
Phone: (503) 378-2053
Fax: (503) 378-8666

Pennsylvania

Bureau of Statistics and Policy Research
Pennsylvania Commission on
  Crime and Delinquency
P.O. Box 1167
Harrisburg, PA 17108
Phone: (717) 787-5152
Fax: (717) 783-7713
WWW: http://www.pccd.state.pa.us

Puerto Rico

Statistical Analysis Center
Criminal Justice Information System
P.O. Box 192
San Juan, PR 00902
Phone: (787) 729-2122
Fax: (787) 729-2261

Rhode Island

Rhode Island Governor's Justice
  Commission
One Capitol Hill, 4th Floor
Providence, RI 02908
Phone: (401) 222-4499
Fax: (401) 222-1294

South Carolina

Planning and Research
South Carolina Department of
  Public Safety
5400 Broad River Road
Columbia, SC 29210
Phone: (803) 896-8717
Fax: (803) 896-8719

South Dakota

Statistical Analysis Center
Office of the Attorney General
500 East Capitol Avenue
Pierre, SD 57501

Phone: (605) 773-6313
Fax: (605) 773-6471

Tennessee

Statistical Analysis Center
Tennessee Bureau of Investigation
1148 Foster Avenue
Nashville, TN 37210
Phone: (615) 726-7970
Fax: (615) 741-4789

Texas

Criminal Justice Policy Council
Stephen F. Austin Building
1700 North Congress, Suite 1029
Austin, TX 78701
Phone: (512) 463-1810
Fax: (512) 475-4843

Utah

Statistical Analysis Center
101 State Capitol
Salt Lake City, UT 84114
Phone: (801) 538-1031
Fax: (801) 538-9609
WWW: http://www.justice.state.ut.us

Vermont

Vermont Center for Justice Research
33 College Street
Montpelier, VT 05602
Phone: (802) 828-8511
Fax: (802) 828-8512
WWW: http://www.norwich.edu/
pubs/djrb

Virginia

Statistical Analysis Center
Department of Criminal Justice Services
805 East Broad Street
Richmond, VA 23219
Phone: (804) 371-2371
Fax: (804) 225-3853

Washington

Office of Financial Management
Statistical Analysis Center

P.O. Box 43113
Olympia, WA 98504
Phone: (360) 902-0528
Fax: (360) 664-8941

West Virginia

Criminal Justice Statistical
    Analysis Center
1204 Kanawha Boulevard, East
Huntington, WV 25301

Phone: (304) 558-8814, ext. 218
Fax: (304) 558-0391

Wisconsin

Statistical Analysis Center
Wisconsin Office of Justice Assistance
222 State Street, 2nd Floor
Madison, WI 53702
Phone: (608) 266-7185
Fax: (608) 266-6676

Appendix B

State Administering Agencies

SAAs, some of which also undertake statewide criminal justice planning, administer federal grant programs, most notably, the Edward Byrne Memorial State and Local Law Enforcement Assistance Program. Grant seekers should contact the SAA in their respective state or territory and get on the mailing list for grant announcements, application materials, and other related documents.

Alabama

Department of Economic and
   Community Affairs
401 Adams Avenue, P.O. Box 5690
Montgomery, AL 36103-5690
Phone: (334) 242-5891
Fax: (334) 242-0712

Alaska

Alaska State Troopers
5700 East Tudor Road
Anchorage, AK 99507
Phone: (907) 269-5082
Fax: (907) 337-2059

American Samoa

Criminal Justice Planning Agency
American Samoa Government
Executive Office Building, 3rd Floor
Pago Pago, AS 96799
Phone: (011) (684) 633-5221
Fax: (011) (684) 633-7894

Arizona

Arizona Criminal Justice Commission
1501 West Washington Street, Suite 207
Phoenix, AZ 85007
Phone: (602) 542-1928
Fax: (602) 542-4852

Arkansas

Office of Intergovernmental Services
Department of Finance and
   Administration
1515 Building, Suite 417
P.O. Box 3278

Little Rock, AR 72203
Phone: (501) 682-1074
Fax: (501) 682-5206

California

Office of Criminal Justice Planning
1130 K Street, Suite 300
Sacramento, CA 95814
Phone: (916) 324-9163
Fax: (916) 327-8714
WWW: http://www.ocjp.ca.gov/

Colorado

Division of Criminal Justice
700 Kipling Street, 3rd Floor
Denver, CO 80215
Phone: (303) 239-4442
Fax: (303) 239-4491
WWW:
http://www.state.co.us/gov_dir/cdps/
    dcj.htm

Connecticut

Office of Policy and Management
450 Capitol Avenue, MS #52CPD
P.O. Box 341441
Hartford, CT 06134-1441
Phone: (860) 418-6210
Fax: (860) 418-6496

Delaware

Criminal Justice Council
Carvel State Office Building
820 North French Street, 4th Floor
Wilmington, DE 19801
Phone: (302) 577-5030
Fax: (302) 577-3440
WWW: http://www.state.de.us/govern/
    agencies/cjc/cjc.htm

District of Columbia

Office of Grants Management
    and Development
717 14th Street, NW, Suite 500
Washington, DC 20005
Phone: (202) 727-6537
Fax: (202) 727-1617

Florida

Department of Community Affairs
2555 Shumard Oak Blvd.
Tallahassee, FL 32399
Phone: (904) 488-8016
Fax: (904) 487-4414

Georgia

Criminal Justice Coordinating Council
503 Oak Place, Suite 540
Atlanta, GA 30349
Phone: (404) 559-4949
Fax: (404) 559-4960

Guam

Bureau of Planning
Governor's Office
P.O. Box 2950
Agana, GU 96910
Phone: (011) (671) 472-4201
Fax: (011) (671) 477-1812

Hawaii

Attorney General
State of Hawaii
425 Queen Street, Room 221
Honolulu, HI 96813
Phone: (808) 586-1151
Fax: (808) 586-1373

Idaho

Idaho Department of Law
    Enforcement
P.O. Box 700
Meridian, ID 83680-0700
Phone: (208) 884-7040
Fax: (208) 884-7094

Illinois

Illinois Criminal Justice
    Information Authority
120 South Riverside Plaza, Suite 1016
Chicago, IL 60606
Phone: (312) 793-8550
Fax: (312) 793-8422
WWW: http://www.icjia.state.il.us/

Indiana

Indiana Criminal Justice Institute
302 West Washington Street,
   Room E-209
Indianapolis, IN 46204
Phone: (317) 232-1230
Fax: (317) 232-4979

Iowa

Governor's Alliance on Substance Abuse
Lucas State Office Building, 2nd Floor
Des Moines, IA 50319
Phone: (515) 281-3788
Fax: (515) 242-6390

Kansas

Kansas Criminal Justice
Coordinating Council
700 Jackson Street, SW, Room 501
Topeka, KS 66603
Phone: (913) 296-0923
Fax: (913) 296-0927

Kentucky

Division of Grants Management
Justice Cabinet
Bush Building
403 Wapping Street, 2nd Floor
Frankfort, KY 40601
Phone: (502) 564-7554
Fax: (502) 564-4840

Louisiana

Louisiana Commission on
   Law Enforcement
1885 Wooddale Blvd., Suite 708
Baton Rouge, LA 70806
Phone: (504) 925-3513
Fax: (504) 925-1998

Maine

Department of Public Safety
State House Station 42
Augusta, ME 04333
Phone: (207) 877-8016
Fax: (207) 624-8768

Maryland

Governor's Office of Crime
   Control and Prevention
300 East Joppa Road, Suite 1105
Baltimore, MD 21286-3016
Phone: (410) 321-3521
Fax: (410) 321-3116
WWW: http://www.bsos.umd.edu/
   cesar/goccp/goccp.html

Massachusetts

Jonathan M. Petuchowski,
   Executive Director
Massachusetts Committee on
   Criminal Justice
100 Cambridge Street, Room 2100
Boston, MA 02202
Phone: (617) 727-6300
Fax: (617) 727-5356

Michigan

Office of Drug Control Policy
Lewis Cass Building, 2nd Floor
320 South Walnut
Lansing, MI 48913
Phone: (517) 373-2952
Fax: (517) 373-2963

Minnesota

Office of Drug Policy and
   Violence Prevention
Department of Public Safety
550 Cedar Street, Suite 409
St. Paul, MN 55101
Phone: (612) 296-0922
Fax: (612) 297-7313 (ODP)

Mississippi

Division of Public Safety Planning
Department of Public Safety
401 North West Street, 8th Floor
P.O. Box 23039
Jackson, MS 39225-3039
Phone: (601) 359-7880
Fax: (601) 359-7832

Missouri

Missouri Department of Public Safety
Truman State Office Building,
  Room 870
P.O. Box 749
Jefferson City, MO 65102-0749
Phone: (573) 751-4905
Fax: (573) 751-5399

Montana

Montana Board of Crime Control
303 North Roberts
Scott Hart Bldg.
Helena, MT 59620
Phone: (406) 444-3604
Fax: (406) 444-4722

Nebraska

Nebraska Commission on Law
  Enforcement and Criminal Justice
301 Centennial Mall South
P.O. Box 94946
Lincoln, NE 68509
Phone: (402) 471-3416
Fax: (402) 471-2837

Nevada

Office of Criminal Justice Assistance
555 Wright Way
Carson City, NV 89711-0900
Phone: (702) 687-5282
Fax: (702) 687-8798

New Hampshire

Office of the Attorney General
33 Capitol Street
Concord, NH 03301
Phone: (603) 271-1297
Fax: (603) 271-2110

New Jersey

Division of Criminal Justice
Department of Law and Public Safety
25 Market Street, CN 085
Trenton, NJ 08625-0085
Phone: (609) 292-5939
Fax: (609) 292-1451

New Mexico

Department of Public Safety
P.O. Box 1628
Santa Fe, NM 87504-1628
Phone: (505) 827-3420
Fax: (505) 827-3398

New York

New York State Division of Criminal
  Justice Services
Executive Park Tower
Stuyvesant Plaza
Albany, NY 12203-3764
Phone: (518) 457-8462
Fax: (518) 457-1186

North Carolina

Governor's Crime Commission
3824 Barrett Drive, Suite 100
Raleigh, NC 27609
Phone: (919) 571-4736
Fax: (919) 571-4745

North Dakota

Bureau of Criminal Investigation
Attorney General's Office
P.O. Box 1054
Bismarck, ND 58502
Phone: (701) 328-5500
Fax: (701) 328-5510

Northern Mariana Islands

Criminal Justice Planning Agency
Commonwealth of the Northern
  Mariana Islands
Office of the Governor
Saipan, MP 96950
Phone: (011) (670) 664-4550
Fax: (011) (670) 664-4560

Ohio

Office of Criminal Justice Services
400 East Town Street, Suite 120
Columbus, OH 43215-4242
Phone: (614) 466-7782
Fax: (614) 466-0308
WWW: http://www.ocjs.state.oh.us/

Oklahoma

District Attorneys Training and
Coordination Council
2200 Classen Blvd., Suite 1800
Oklahoma City, OK 73106-5811
Phone: (405) 557-6707
Fax: (405) 524-0581

Oregon

Oregon Department of State Police
Criminal Justice Services Division
400 Public Service Building
Salem, OR 97310
Phone: (503) 378-3720
Fax: (503) 378-6993

Pennsylvania

Pennsylvania Commission on Crime
and Delinquency
P.O. Box 1167, Federal Square Station
Harrisburg, PA 17108-1167
Phone: (717) 787-8559, ext. 3064
Fax: (717) 783-7713

Puerto Rico

Attorney General
Department of Justice
Commonwealth of Puerto Rico
P.O. Box 9020192
San Juan, PR 00902-0192
Phone: (787) 725-0335
Fax: (787) 725-6144

Rhode Island

Governor's Justice Commission
One Capitol Hill, 4th Floor
Providence, RI 02908-5803
Phone: (401) 222-2620
Fax: (401) 222-1294

South Carolina

Office of Safety and Grants
Department of Public Safety
5400 Broad River Road
Columbia, SC 29210-4088
Phone: (803) 896-8707
Fax: (803) 896-8714

South Dakota

Attorney General's Task Force on Drugs
State Capitol Building
500 East Capitol Avenue
Pierre, SD 57501-5070
Phone: (605) 773-6313
Fax: (605) 773-6471

Tennessee

Office of Criminal Justice Programs
Department of Finance and
Administration
1400 Andrew Jackson Building
500 Deaderick Street
Nashville, TN 37243-1700
Phone: (615) 532-2986
Fax: (615) 532-2989

Texas

Criminal Justice Division
Office of the Governor
P.O. Box 12428, Capitol Station
Austin, TX 78711
Phone: (512) 463-1806
Fax: (512) 475-2440

Utah

Commission on Criminal and
Juvenile Justice
State Capitol Building, Room 101
Salt Lake City, UT 84114
Phone: (801) 538-1031
Fax: (801) 538-1024

Vermont

Vermont Department of Public Safety
Waterbury State Complex
103 South Main Street
Waterbury, VT 05676-0850
Phone: (802) 244-8781
Fax: (802) 244-1106

Virginia

Department of Criminal Justice Services
805 East Broad Street, 10th Floor
Richmond, VA 23219
Phone: (804) 786-1577
Fax: (804) 371-8981

Virgin Islands

Virgin Islands Law Enforcement
Planning Commission
8172 Submarine Base, Suite 3
Estate Nisky #6 Southside Quarters
St. Thomas, VI 00802
Phone: (809) 774-6400
Fax: (809) 776-3317

Washington

Washington State Department of
    Community, Trade and Economic
    Development
906 Columbia Street, SW
P.O. Box 48300
Olympia, WA 98504
Phone: (360) 586-8411
Fax: (360) 586-0489

West Virginia

Office of Criminal Justice and
    Highway Safety
Department of Military Affairs
    and Public Safety
1204 Kanawha Blvd., East
Charleston, WV 25301
Phone: (304) 558-8814, ext. 215
Fax: (304) 558-0391

Wisconsin

Wisconsin Office of Justice Assistance
222 State Street, 2nd Floor
Madison, WI 53702
Phone: (608) 266-7282
Fax: (608) 266-6676

Wyoming

Division of Criminal Investigation
316 West 22nd Street
Cheyenne, WY 82002
Phone: (307) 777-7181
Fax: (307) 777-7252

Appendix C

Sample Program Proposal

The following sample of a direct service program proposal was created for illustration. The names, affiliations, and references all are fictitious. This example does, however, show how the elements of a program proposal come together into a unified "story" of a real-world criminal justice problem.

SERIAL CRIMINAL APPREHENSION TACTIC (SCAT)

Abstract

The Metro-Franklin Police Department proposes to use National Incident-Based Reporting System (NIBRS) data to identify and apprehend serial offenders. NIBRS data offer a detailed picture of individual crime incidents, enabling the crime analyst to perform complex, multivariate analyses of offender, victim, crime scene, and property characteristics. Because they are geocoded, these data can also be mapped. The proposed project involves the immediate, in-depth analysis of NIBRS data for commonalities that can link them to serial offenders. The immediate turnaround of mapped, serial crime data is expected to allow law enforcement authorities to visually track each incident when reported. This, in turn, will enable authorities to identify possible crime series early in the series. Early identification of crime series will facilitate earlier apprehension of predatory serial offenders, thereby reducing victimization in Metropolitan Franklin County.

Problem Statement

Serial murderers, rapists, and arsonists are responsible for a disproportionate amount of predatory crime in the Metropolitan Franklin County area (Miller, 1998). Within the past 10 years, local law enforcement agencies have identified 17 serial offenders. Although all but 3 were eventually identified and apprehended, together they were responsible for 243 known offenses. These included 41 homicides, 176 sexual assaults, and 26 cases of arson.

Such staggering numbers do not reveal the extent of the human misery wrought by such offenders. The Victim-Witness Program reveals that for every serial offender, the office receives no fewer than six referrals (Baxter, 1998). Often, these are the so-called secondary victims—relatives and friends of those who were murdered or assaulted. The victim toll of these offenders also includes owners of residential and commercial property destroyed by the serial arsonists.

In addition to the untold emotional devastation wreaked by these offenders, they cost the local criminal justice system millions of dollars. The Metro-Franklin Police Department alone estimates its investigatory and court time for these cases during the past 5 years at $840,000 (Shaw, 1997). The estimated disposition costs of all these offenses total more than $2.5 million (Chambers, 1998).

The Federal Bureau of Investigation's Violent Criminal Apprehension Program (VICAP) was designed to help law enforcement across the country combat violent, predatory crime. The original design called for law enforcement agencies across the United States to contribute detailed information on homicide, sexual assault, and arson cases to the VICAP database. The FBI would then regularly and systematically search for patterns and other common characteristics in the hopes of identifying such offenses and offenders early on in their series (Rollins, 1987).

For possible serial crimes to be contributed to the VICAP computerized database, the contributing law enforcement agency must complete a detailed, 14-page questionnaire. The information from this questionnaire is then entered into the FBI's VICAP computer system. Every day, the FBI computer searches the entered cases for commonalities. Cases with similar characteristics may then warrant further investigation.

Despite the strong conceptual underpinnings, VICAP has not worked as originally intended. Although several states have developed programs similar to

VICAP, the majority of law enforcement agencies across the United States do not voluntarily contribute crime data (Wakefield, 1995). This effectively eliminates the possibility of tracking serial offenders, many of whom do not offend within specific geographical boundaries (Sellers, 1997). Consequently, the VICAP system cannot adequately serve the needs of Metro-Franklin and surrounding areas.

Methods

The Metro-Franklin Police Department's Crime Analysis Unit proposes to implement a new program known as the Serial Criminal Apprehension Tactic (SCAT). This will involve hiring a crime analyst whose sole responsibility will be to search for serial crime patterns. The crime analyst will use an IBM-compatible computer to systematically analyze crime patterns in the county crime data. The crime analyst and new equipment will be housed in a secure office within the county administration complex. The program will also require a new, full-time data entry specialist who will immediately enter crime incident forms into the department's NIBRS database.

Once each morning, the crime analyst will meet with experienced detectives from the homicide, sexual assault, and arson squads. The analyst will discuss any and all patterns recently identified. These patterns will take the form of color maps that show the location of similar homicide, sex, and arson offenses.

When the analyst and detectives are confident that they have identified a possible series, they will generate a list of possible suspects. This list will consist of persons who are known to local law enforcement agencies for having been charged with, or suspected of, qualifying offenses within the past 5 years. The list will also include those persons who are known to live near the crime scenes who fit the profile of either organized or disorganized serial offenders.

On the basis of previous serial crime investigations, such early identification of possible suspects leads to, in the majority of cases, identification and apprehension of the offender responsible for the series in question (Fuller, 1990). The proposed project, then, will save countless hours of investigative time spent on erroneous leads. More important, however, SCAT will result in a significant reduction of victimization by these serial offenders.

Objectives

The proposed project has several objectives for the first year of operation. Each of these is detailed below.

Objective 1: Beginning with the second month of the project period, the proposed project will produce daily lists of possible serial crimes.

Currently, the department does not generate any lists of qualifying crimes. This project will result in no fewer than 335 such lists for the entire project period.

Objective 2: Beginning with the second month of the project period, the proposed project will produce and distribute location maps of possible serial crimes.

Currently, the department does not generate any maps of serial crimes. Maps will be distributed to patrol officers at roll call each day during the project period.

Objective 3: We will reduce the time between identification of a violent crime series and apprehension of a suspect by 25% within the project period.

This objective will be assessed by comparing the time intervals of cases during the project period with serial cases solved prior to the implementation of this project. Previously, the mean time from identification to apprehension for homicide, sexual assault, and arson cases was 13 months, 2 weeks.

Budget

Personnel
Crime Analyst, 2,080 hours @ $19.65 per hour	$40,872
Benefits @ 28% of total salary	$11,444
Data Entry Clerk, 2,080 hours @ $11.80 per hour	$24,544
Benefits @ 28% of total salary	$6,872
Personnel subtotal	$83,732

Equipment
Personal computer, 1 @ $2,495	$2,495
Color mapping printer, 1 @ $729	$729
Equipment subtotal	$3,224

Travel
Airfare to Washington, D.C.	$280
Per diem, 3 days @ $175 per day	$525
Travel subtotal	$805

Contractual Items
Computer and printer maintenance contract @ $125 per year	$125

Consultants
Richard Righteous, 30 hours @ $35 per hour	$1,050
Budget total	$88,936

Budget Narrative

Personnel
The salary for both positions reflects the current rate of pay plus the upcoming raise currently being negotiated by the bargaining unit. Benefits, calculated for all

department employees at 28% of salary, include health insurance, workers' compensation, dental benefits, and prepaid legal services.

Equipment

This project will require a state-of-the-art Pentium computer capable of multiple tasks including statistical analyses, mapping, database management, word processing, and presentation. The estimated cost comes from the department's term contract with DataLaw, Inc. The printer, also listed by term contract price, is necessary to print complex, colored crime maps.

Travel

Ms. Samuels will be traveling round-trip to the annual meeting of the Homicide Investigators' Roundtable meeting in Washington, D.C. There she will attend advanced sessions on the analysis of NIBRS data for serial crime investigation. The per diem is the normal amount allowed for lodging, meals, and related incidental expenses.

Contractual Items

This contract, with InfoFix, Inc., will cover both regular and emergency maintenance of the computer and printer for 1 year.

Consultants

Richard Righteous will advise the project staff on the analysis of serial crime data. This hourly rate, which is the rate he customarily charges law enforcement agencies, includes his travel, hotel, and other business expenses.

Capability Statement

Organizational Capability

The Metro-Franklin Police Department has been in operation for the past 110 years. It consists of patrol, detective, identification, research and planning, and traffic bureaus. As of January of this year, the department employed 305 staff members, 260 of whom are sworn police officers.

The department has embraced the philosophy embodied in the principles of community policing. This resulted in a restructuring of the department that flattened the pyramidal hierarchy and replaced it with 16 neighborhood substations, each of which is more or less autonomous. Since adopting community policing, the Metro-Franklin area has experienced an overall decrease in both violent and property crime. Specifically, within the past 3 years, Part I violent crimes have dropped by 17%, and Part I property crimes have diminished by 24%. Although other factors may have played a part in these declines, the department is confident that community policing is responsible for most of it.

Within the past 5 years, the department has been awarded 13 discretionary grants from state and federal agencies. The amounts of these grants have ranged from $8,500 to $282,000. All required fiscal and programmatic reports have been submitted on time. Moreover, in all but one grant, the projects met or exceeded all their objectives. Three of these funded projects were awarded "exemplary status" by the federal Office of Exemplary Criminal Justice Projects.

Staff Qualifications

Kendra Samuels, crime analyst for the proposed project, holds the B.A. and M.A. degrees in criminology and criminal justice from the University of Maryland at College Park. Currently, she is graduate research associate at the Institute for Juvenile Research in Chicago. In addition to her university course work, Ms. Samuels has taken advanced workshops in data mapping from the Justice Research and Statistics Association and a course on the analysis of NIBRS data at the University of Michigan's Institute for Social Research. She participates in the Homicide Investigators' Roundtable, which holds annual conferences centering on the study of murder.

Richard Righteous, consultant to the proposed project, is a former profiler with the FBI's Behavioral Sciences Unit in Quantico, Virginia. He has conducted in-depth research on serial offenders, the results of which have been published in the *Journal of Interpersonal Violence, Violence and Victims, FBI Law Enforcement Bulletin,* and many other professional and scholarly journals. He holds a doctorate in clinical psychology from Georgetown University. Since 1977, he has consulted in more than 400 serial crime investigations. Now retired from the FBI, Dr. Righteous is President of MonsterMash, a private consulting firm dedicated to helping law enforcement identify and apprehend violent, predatory offenders.

References

Baxter, H. J. (1998). Serial murderers account for disproportionate amount of crime. *The Law Enforcer, 9*(2), 107-122.

Chambers, M. (1998). Serial cases break the bank. In R. Ganz (Ed.), *Murder in America.* La Jolla Park, CA: Policy Publications.

Fuller, J. Q. (1990). Identifying serial offenders: The benefits of early detection. In R. Meriweather (Ed.), *Violence in the United States.* New York: Academician's Press.

Miller, J. (1998, August 12). Serial murderers frustrating authorities. *Metro-Franklin Mirror-Times,* pp. A1-A2.

Rollins, P. (1987). VICAP: Its history, purpose and potential. In V. Humboldt (Ed.), *Technology in the fight against crime.* Cincinnati, OH: Forthright.

Sellers, J. R. (1997). The spatial considerations of serial crime. *Journal of Applied Criminology, 7*(3), 58-71.

Shaw, K. E. (1997). *Serial cases breaking the bank: Special report to the Metro-Franklin Commissioners.* Franklin City, OH: Metro-Franklin Department of Public Safety.

Wakefield, J. (1995). VICAP's promising potential compromised. *American Journal of Homicide Studies, 4*(2), 32-51.

Appendix D

Sample Research Proposal

This sample was based on an actual proposal. The names, affiliations, and references are, however, mostly fictitious.

ELITE DEVIANCE AND LABELING THEORY:
A TEST USING WAYWARD SCIENTISTS

Abstract

A number of investigators have examined deviant behavior in science. Previous studies have focused on the various forms of deviant behavior by scientists, as well as on the incidence of such behavior. Theoretical work in the field, however, lags behind the empirical work. One facet not yet explored by previous research is the effect of labeling on scientists who have been found guilty of engaging in scientific misconduct. Fraud in science, for example, considered the most serious crime of science, is said to bring about severe responses from peers and employers, as well as from the sponsors of scientific research.

The proposed study will explore the extent to which scientists who have been found guilty of lab-coat crime are labeled by institutions of social control. Data for this project will be gathered through interviews with scientists who have been found guilty of plagiarism or the falsification of data. These interview data will be supplemented by an examination of official documents of the ethical misconduct proceedings and by interviews with former employers of these wayward scientists. The textual material will be quantitatively analyzed using CONTEXT content analysis software.

Introduction

Once criminology embraced Sutherland's (1940) concept of white-collar crime, criminology expanded these inquiries well beyond the corporate world and its profits. The scandal in the 1970s known as Watergate became a symbol of the legal and ethical breaches of the political world. At about the same time, corporations such as Boeing and Dow were suspected of blatant disregard of the sanctity of human life. Even prominent members of the clergy became embroiled in scandals that brought them down in disgrace. Elite crime and deviance, it was discovered, had many forms and found expression in many arenas.

Sociologist of science Thompson (1951) was among the first to explore the notion of deviant behavior in science. Violations that Thompson called "laboratory indiscretions" were used to describe deviant—perhaps even criminal—behavior that could be endemic to the scientific profession.

Feinstein (1963), in his essay on deviant behavior in science, discussed several ways in which scientists breach scientific norms. One major form of norm violation in science is plagiarism. Other forms include the falsification of data, regarded by Feinstein as science's most reprehensible offense. In this review article, he attempts to apply several of the more popular theoretical perspectives on deviant behavior. None is found to explain scientific misconduct satisfactorily.

Neither Thompson nor Feinstein gave lengthy discussion in their works to the application of the labeling perspective to scientific misconduct. Inasmuch as Thompson's writing on the norms of science predated much of the work on labeling theory, that is to be expected. It is curious, however, that Feinstein, in his inventory of theoretical perspectives on deviant behavior in science, failed to explore labeling theory in any detail.

The labeling perspective does not purport to explain primary deviance. That is, it is not concerned with establishing etiology for those who originally engage in deviant behavior. Instead, labeling theory is more concerned with the consequences that the labeling process has for those to whom the label of deviant has been successfully applied.

The proposed inquiry, then, intends to explore several related theoretical questions deriving from the labeling perspective. The first has to do with establishing that labeling occurs as a result of social control in academic science. The literature to date says little about the labeling of those who have been found guilty of engaging in ethical misconduct. In instances in which scientists are found to be guilty of the falsification of data, plagiarism, or other forms of scientific norm violation, is an identifiable label actually applied to the individual? In academic science, who performs this labeling process? Can these labels be substantiated using agency records and other archival data?

The second question of interest in the proposed study deals with the consequences of any label that might be applied as a result of informal or formal social control. That is, what is the negative impact, if any, of having been labeled as a plagiarist or data falsifier? Is the individual so labeled cut off from significant professional or career opportunities? Is the individual no longer able to apply for grant monies? How do prospective employers view those who have been found guilty of scientific misconduct?

The proposed project, then, will explore the following hypotheses on the labeling of wayward scientists:

- Scientists labeled as deviant early in their careers are more likely than their established counterparts to suffer from the effects of labeling.
- The more prestigious the institution in which the alleged misconduct occurs, the less harmful are the effects of labeling.
- Scientists with crossover credentials (e.g., M.D.) are less likely to suffer from the effects of labeling than are those with nonprofessional, terminal degrees (e.g., Ph.D.).

Methods

Sample

The participants for this study will be identified from the list of all those whose cases of scientific misconduct have been published in the *Federal Register,* the publication of the U.S. Government Printing Office that appears every weekday except holidays. In the *Federal Register,* the Department of Health and Human Services (DHHS) publishes those cases of scientific misconduct in which the Office of Research Integrity has made a finding against an alleged offender. The notice reveals the scientist's name, affiliation, and the type of misconduct of which he or she has been found guilty. The proposed study will include all cases published in the *Federal Register* from January 1994 through December 1998.

The population for this study, then, will consist of all scientists who have been listed in the *Federal Register* as having a finding of scientific misconduct against them. Each of these scientists will be contacted to determine if he or she will agree to an interview. It is expected that not all scientists in the population will be located. Further, it is possible, if not probable, that not all those contacted will agree to interviews.

In selected cases in which the participant lives in proximity to the principal investigator, the interview will be conducted in person. In most cases, the interview will take place via telephone. With the interviewee's permission, the interview will be tape-recorded. The first phase of data collection, then, will involve semistructured interviews with the labeled scientists. A semistructured interview schedule will ensure that comparable data are collected from all study participants. This process will permit the interviewer to pursue additional inquiries based on the information provided by the interviewee. The structured portion of the data for this interview schedule will include but not necessarily be limited to the following:

- Age
- Sex
- Race/ethnicity
- Highest degree earned
- Year degree earned
- Institution from which highest degree earned
- Field of study of highest degree
- Affiliation at time of accusation
- Affiliation at time of alleged misconduct
- Narrative explanation of incident

In the second phase of the study, the researcher team will collect data from the institution with which the scientist was affiliated when he or she engaged in scientific misconduct. Of interest here is the extent to which archival sources or persons other than the accused reveal information about the possible labeling of the scientist in question. Data elements for the Phase II Questionnaire will include but not necessarily be limited to the following:

- Institution from which data are secured
- Is scientist eligible for rehire?
- Do official records verify the alleged misconduct?
- Do official records verify contacts by employers subsequent to alleged misconduct?
- Press coverage of incident
- Sponsoring agency (e.g., NSF, NIH) decision on alleged misconduct
- Sponsoring agency notice in *Federal Register*

- Criminal prosecution status
- Measure of the institution's grant activity (number of grants, amounts, etc.)

The quantitative data will be entered into an SPSS data file. The textual material, which includes narrative statements of the scientists under study, as well as those of knowledgeable parties such as former employers and research colleagues, will be keyed and subsequently analyzed using CONTEXT software, which is designed specifically for content analysis.

Methods of Analysis

The analysis of the data will consist first of an examination of frequencies of the variables. In subsequent bivariate analyses, which will take the form of cross tabulations, the research team will look for evidence that the labeling of scientists had negative consequences. This will be revealed by the comparison of the scientists' position and salary with what they report they would have had in the absence of a guilty finding by DHHS.

These data will be further analyzed, controlling for various individual and institutional variables detailed above. This will be accomplished by log-linear analysis and logistic regression.

Once analyzed, the data will be presented at the upcoming annual meetings of the American Sociological Association and the American Association for the Advancement of Science. The research team also intends to submit the results of the proposed project to appropriate scholarly journals.

Budget

Personnel

Project Director, 2,080 hours @ $37.85 per hour	$78,728
Benefits @ 34% of total salary	$26,768
Graduate Research Assistant, 1,040 hours @ $11.80 per hour	$12,272
Benefits @ 34% of total salary	$4,172
Personnel subtotal	$121,940

Equipment

Transcribing tape recorder, 1 @ $395	$395

Supplies

Audiotapes, 50 @ $2.00 per tape	$100

Travel

Round-trip airfare to ASA and AAAS meetings	$960
Auto mileage, 1,500 miles @ $.32 per mile	$480
Travel subtotal	$1,440

Contractual Items

Not applicable	

Consultants

Richard Righteous, 30 hours @ $35 per hour	$1,050
Budget total	$124,925

Budget Narrative

Personnel

Dr. Norman Greenleaf, Project Director and Principal Investigator, will work full-time on this project. The 34% for employee benefits is the university's customary rate and includes health insurance coverage, life insurance, workers' compensation and disability benefits, and contributions to the State Instructors' Retirement System.

Nora Fairchild, Graduate Research Assistant, will spend 50% of her time on this project. Full-time graduate student benefits are calculated by the university at the same rate as faculty and staff. These include all coverages listed above.

Equipment

The transcribing tape recorder will permit Dr. Greenleaf to record and later have transcribed the detailed interviews with the project's participants. The price reflects the lowest of three bids for this equipment.

Supplies

This amount consists of only 50 audiotapes, which will be purchased at a local discount office supply warehouse.

Travel

Dr. Greenleaf will make presentations at the annual meetings of the American Sociological Association and the American Association for the Advancement of Science. His hotel and meal expenses for these meetings will be covered by another grant under which he is making other presentations.

Contractual Items

Not applicable

Consultants

Dr. Righteous will consult on the analysis of textual data. The hourly fee is his customary charge for statistical and methodological consultation.

Organizational Capability and Staffing

Organizational Capability

The State University of Northern Virginia opened its doors in 1870. It consists of an undergraduate college and 16 other academic subdivisions offering undergraduate, graduate, and professional education. The university has been listed in *Public Gothic,* a compilation of those institutions of higher learning in which the quality of education is comparable with the great universities.

Currently, the University Research Foundation manages 82 grants and cooperative agreements awarded by such organizations as the National Science Foundation, the National Institute of Justice, the National Institutes of Health, and many other funding agencies and organizations. All programmatic and fiscal reports are submitted on time or early. Neither the university nor any of its faculty or staff has been debarred from applying for or receiving grants.

The Science Study Center, opened in 1985, has served as the university's focal point for the sociological study of the scientific professions. As a center, it now has 22 faculty affiliated as research associates. Current, active research grants and cooperative agreements, which have been awarded by such agencies as the National Science Foundation and the National Institutes of Health, now total more than $1.6 million.

Staff Qualifications

Dr. Norman Greenleaf will serve as Principal Investigator and Project Director. He holds the Ph.D. in sociology with distinction from Columbia University. For the past 8 years, he has served as Director of the Science Study Center at the State University of Northern Virginia. His research on the sociology of science has appeared in *Science, Technology and Human Values, American Journal of Sociology,* and *Social Forces.* He is recent past president of the National Society for the Study of Science and is currently Editor-in-Chief of its quarterly, *Scientists on Science.*

Nora Fairchild, ABD, is Graduate Research Associate at the Science Study Center. She holds the B.A. and M.A. degrees in sociology from the University of Delaware, where she graduated with honors in 1998.

REFERENCES

Feinstein, J. (1963). Departures from scientific norms. *Northwestern Sociological Review, 21*(4), 37-53.
Sutherland, E. H. (1940). White-collar criminality. *American Sociological Review, 5,* 1-12.
Thompson, J. P. (1951). Laboratory indiscretions in the conduct of scientific research. *Annals of Western Science, 97*(5), 32-39.

Appendix E

For Further Reading

The following books are additional sources of information on grants and grantsmanship. The reader is encouraged to go beyond the introduction offered in this work and to learn as much as possible about the process of securing grants. Although these titles do not speak specifically to criminal justice professionals, each offers unique advice that grant seekers should add to their toolboxes.

Bauer, D. G. (1984). *The "how to" grants manual.* New York: Macmillan.

Coley, S. M., & Scheinberg, C. A. (1990). *Proposal writing.* Newbury Park, CA: Sage.

Conrad, D. L. (1980). *The quick proposal workbook.* San Francisco: Public Management Institute.

Frost, G. J. (1993). *Winning grant proposals.* Rockville, MD: Fund Raising Institute.

Gilpatrick, E. (1989). *Grants for nonprofit organizations: A guide to funding and grant writing.* New York: Praeger.

Hall, M. S. (1988). *Getting funded: A complete guide to proposal writing.* Portland, OR: Portland State University, Continuing Education Publications.

Keegan, P. B. (1990). *Fundraising for non-profits.* New York: HarperCollins.

Kiritz, N. J. (1980). *Program planning & proposal writing.* Los Angeles: Grantsmanship Center.

Lauffer, A. (1984). *Grantsmanship and fund raising.* Beverly Hills, CA: Sage.

Lefferts, R. (1990). *Getting a grant in the 1990s: How to write successful grant proposals.* New York: Simon & Schuster/Fireside.

Locke, L. F., Spirduso, W. W., & Silverman, S. J. (1987). *Proposals that work: A guide for planning dissertations and grant proposals* (2nd ed.). Newbury Park, CA: Sage.

Margolin, J. B. (1983). *The individual's guide to grants.* New York: Plenum.

Masterman, L. E. (1978). *The applicant's guide to successful grantsmanship.* Cape Girardeau, MO: Keene.

Nauffts, M. F. (1994). *Foundation fundamentals: A guide for grantseekers* (5th ed.). New York: Foundation Center.

Schumacher, D. (1992). *Get funded! A practical guide for scholars seeking research support from business.* Newbury Park, CA: Sage.

Index

Wisconsin:
  SAAs, 108
  SACs, 102
Word processing equipment, access to, 33-34.
  See also Computers
World Wide Web:
  access, 33

home page links, 20
private foundation home pages, 16
research and, 31
state agency home pages, 94
  See also Internet
Wyoming:
  SAAs, 108

About the Author

Mark S. Davis is Chief Criminologist in Ohio's Office of Criminal Justice Services. He holds BA, MA, and PhD degrees from The Ohio State University, where he occasionally teaches criminology. Grant proposals he has authored or coauthored have resulted in awards from the Bureau of Justice Assistance, the Bureau of Justice Statistics, the National Institute of Justice, the National Science Foundation, the Office of Criminal Justice Services, and the Office of Juvenile Justice and Delinquency Prevention. His research has appeared in the *Journal of Criminal Justice, Social Justice Research,* and *Policing: An International Journal of Police Strategies and Management.*